REMEMBERING SELF

Seasons of the Soul Rediscovered Through Mystical Experience and Depth Psychology

ADVANCE PRAISE

Remembering Self has many unexpected messages. In a world which seems to be drowning in nonsense of its own making, leaving many struggling with confusion about death, dying and the hereafter, *Remembering Self* will surely be a wondrous and welcome surprise. Dr. Lakritz declares with a clear, decisive, and firm voice his assumptions, beliefs, and insights. These insights are compelling and, whether you embrace them or not, are likely to provoke new ways of seeing and thinking about your life.

Dr. Lakritz explains that re-membering can be viewed as a process of re-collecting the experiences of a lifetime, like the weaving of patterns on a garment whose form, if we look closely enough, over time begins to coalesce into meaningful images. Looking back after reading *Remembering Self* was transformative in embracing a deeper appreciation of life emerging as a direct connection to being in the present moment.

When I finished reading this memorable and important book, the words of D.T. Suzuki surfaced and helped define my experience: "I have been reading all day and remaining in my room...I move the chair and look at the Blue Mountains...I fill my lungs and am refreshed. I make tea and drink a cup...Who would say I am not living in the light of eternity?"

— Leonard M. Zunin, MD, Psychiatrist, Author & Artist

Through three different voices — the transcendently wise Cornelius; the dying elder, Shemah; and the witnessing Author — *Remembering Self* helps us to navigate what the author calls "the great labyrinth of life." Describing human development in four "seasons," Dr. Lakritz artfully shows how each season is a foundational stage in the journey toward realization of our essential being. He presents a clear philosophical and psychological roadmap that allows anyone on a conscious journey to recognize and follow through the twists and turns of life."

— Rajashree Maa (Joni Dittrich, PhD), Teacher and Author,
May the Loveforce Be With You — Kali-Ki Reiki:
Healing Through Divine Mother & Yogic Wisdom

What we see in the story presented beautifully by Dr. Lakritz is the journey of transcendence from the darkness and density of a human incarnation into a remembering and knowing the amazing and infinite dimensionality of the soul in perfect connection with all that is. We are not a drop of water in the vast ocean but rather the ocean in a drop of water. This paradox seems incomprehensible from within the conscious mind, yet, with transcendence, one can simply be the ocean in all of its magnificence. Shemah's journeys of sacred re-membering give a powerful insight into his experience that can inspire others to be engaged in their own journeys of loving experience, remembering, and knowing. Hopefully, this book will inspire you to feel and know your own magnificence in this life and beyond.

— Dr. Diana Paque, Executive Director of the Newton Institute

Shemah and Cornelius, in Dr. Lakritz's embodied writing, do not endeavor to tell us the meaning of life. Countless writers have fallen deeply in love with their versions of the meaning of life and attempted to enroll us into their version and vision. Instead, Dr. Lakritz and his cast of characters guide us how to make meaning of life. This meditation on time, consciousness, and Self is a masterclass in learning how to look below the surface and beyond the obvious, and live intentionally, courageously, and lovingly.

— Eric Kaufmann, CEO of Sagatica, Author of *The Four Virtues of a Leader* and *Leadership Breakdown*

In *Remembering Self*, Dr. Kenneth R. Lakritz masterfully goes beyond simple storytelling to offer us a guide through the intricate pathways of self-discovery. With profound insight, he delineates human development across four distinct "seasons," providing a philosophical and psychological framework that serves not only patients but also all who engage with the complexities of the human psyche professionally. This book delivers a unique perspective into the core of our being, merging psychoanalytic theory with years of therapeutic practices in ways that echo my own experiences in academia and psychiatric care. *Remembering Self* is transformative; it challenges us to reflect on our evolutionary path and reconnect with the essence of who we are. This text is a fantastic resource for mental health professionals, educators, and basically anyone navigating the maze of the human mind and spirit.

— Pedro Zuzarte, MD, PhD, Psychiatrist

Remembering Self is a fine handbook for souls who have incarnated into this earth plane and a guidebook for those who desire to — an inspiring reminder that there are no victims in the universe.

— Reverend Xavier Eikerenkoetter, Author, *Reverend Ike*

You are here on planet Earth to awaken your soul. Your soul is bigger than you are. Your soul deserves your recognizing and realizing its fullest dimensionality. Dr. Ken's brilliant book will get you in high flight to ultimate awareness of your purpose in this earth.

— Mark Victor Hansen, Author, *Chicken Soup for the Soul*

Remembering Self is a guide to the many forms of love that empower us to search for our authentic self. Read it!

— Sam Keen, Author, *To Love and Be Loved*

The term "Self" is not only at the core of Carl Jung's depth psychology but also, in a much broader sense, denotes a basic concept in most spiritual wisdom traditions. Dr. Lakritz is one of the few contemporary Jungians who straddle the worlds of deep philosophical insight and direct therapeutic work with people "on the ground."

"Remembering Self" — the re-connection or re-ligion with who we are at the core of our being — is indispensable, lest we risk getting lost completely in depression, addiction, meaninglessness, and divisiveness.

Dr. Lakritz has issued a staunch reminder, based on decades of personal experience as a dedicated therapist, that we are well advised to humble ourselves and learn that the "self" or ego is at best a "complex" (Jung) that needs to be embedded in the truth of the Self.

— Mark Seelig PhD, Clinical Psychotherapist, Author, *The Self as the Realm of Divine Experience: A Comparison of Carl Jung and Paul Tillich* (published in German language)

Dr. Lakritz has made a significant contribution to the field of consciousness. *Remembering Self* provides the reader with a marvelous and, at times, poetic overview of the ways in which we can integrate different aspects of our being to assist the soul's journey to a deeper understanding of one's purpose in life.

— Thomas Knoblauch, PhD, Author, Elders on Love

Remembering Self is a modern-day masterpiece that illuminates the full capacity of our human experience. Ken is a living embodiment of wisdom, clarity, and heart. His decades of guiding people, leaders and organizations is offered in a way that goes straight to our soul and ignites our sacred evolution…profoundly. You won't be just reading about discovering Self. You will uncover and find *your* Self, which is the most valuable gift to give to oneself and society.

— Satyen Raja, Author, Accelerated Evolution

This book extends a beautiful invitation to rediscover the essence of our being — an exquisite journey through the changing seasons of life. Dr. Lakritz illuminates a path towards greater heartfulness, presence, and understanding of the intricate complexities and mysteries of life. *Remembering Self* is a compelling read that inspires introspection and encourages us to embark on our own inner odyssey. This stunning work will stir your soul.

— Shelley Murphy, PhD, Author, Fostering Mindfulness

REMEMBERING SELF

Seasons of the Soul Rediscovered Through Mystical Experience and Depth Psychology

Eldering Guidance for the Labyrinth of Life and Beyond

Kenneth R. Lakritz, Ph.D.

Books may be purchased through booksellers or by contacting Sacred Stories Publishing.

Cover, Chapter Title & Mandala Illustrations by Nicholas Caan

Remembering Self
Seasons of the Soul Rediscovered Through Mystical Experience and Depth Psychology

Kenneth R. Lakritz, Ph.D.

Print ISBN: 978-1-958921-84-5
EBook ISBN: 978-1-958921-86-9
Library of Congress Control Number: 2026932664

Published by Light on Light Press
An imprint of Sacred Stories Publishing, Fort Lauderdale, FL

Printed in the United States of America

GRATITUDE TO

Carl Jung, Edward Edinger, Erich Neumann, Huston Smith, Ram Dass, Fr. Bede Griffiths, Fr. Dunstan Morrissey and many other elders who have left behind breadcrumbs of wisdom to guide us in our encounters with the Self.

Chakryyuha

We are put on earth - a little place
That we may learn
to bear the beams of love

— William Blake

CONTENTS

ROADMAP

As above,

so below,

as within,

so without,

as the universe,

so the soul.

— Ancient Hermetic Wisdom

There are those who believe that, when the universe was formed, the light emanating from the ground of all being became progressively diluted as it descended into what we have come to conceive as the material world. It is thought that, for this light to be contained within matter and cultivated, it must first be veiled; otherwise, the overwhelming power of the light would shatter the physical vessel into a million pieces.

Because the light of being is veiled, and, therefore, very subtle in the "physical" dimension, it is difficult to perceive. It must be discovered in stages that progressively, and carefully, peel away the veil that appears to separate us from the Essence within which this light originates. Over the course of a lifetime, this process requires numerous, often agonizing, experiences of disassembling and reassembling the structures of life and identity that keep us afloat as we sail the currents of our uncharted destinies. Each stage of Self-discovery that calls us, first, to differentiate from the source of being to establish an earthbound, human identity, and later, to return to be re-united with the ground of who we are has its own distinctive physiology, psychology, and spirituality. Therefore, each phase of life must be understood and approached in terms of its unique qualities and parameters. While the process of the whole of life is certainly greater than the sums of its parts, the particulars of each microcosmic, developmental step make possible openings to deeper being as the foundations of each life stage are formed and consolidated.

Philosophy, psychology, religion, and medicine have been grappling with the attempt to understand the nature of consciousness for millennia. There has been a slow progression toward a unified understanding of the process by which consciousness is formed and informed by our emergent relationship with Self. This work provides a metaphysical and metapsychological framework, a world-view, a unique lens through which we can view the process, purpose, and meaning of the human journey. Within this frame, the intention is to honor the unique, sacred purpose of each individual life and the distinct perspective that grows within it. While I believe that there is a universal structure that underlies the manner in which awareness unfolds within human life, it is through living, experiencing, and exploring that we actually come to meet the One who is us, who took the plunge into matter, into human life, to find adventure within the rich textures of physical existence.

It has been over 35 years since I first felt "called" to engage this current work. Twenty years later, I finally felt mature enough to begin writing. It wasn't until age 66, 16 years later, as I approached the completion of this manuscript, that I finally began to more fully unpack and understand what I had written. The journey of writing this book has been as mystical as it has been intellectual and personal.

Along the way, and after I had finished most of *Remembering Self*, I began to see parallels in both ancient and modern views of *incarnation, emergence*, and *re-integration*. I have come across analogues embodied in many ancient traditions, including Egyptian hermetic, Platonic, Hindu, Kabbalistic, Alchemical, Gnostic, Buddhist, Sufi, and Taoist mystical perspectives.

Early in the twentieth century, beginning with Freud's notion of (adaptive or therapeutic) *regression in service of the ego*, the idea of emergent consciousness with its transformative and healing properties was a revolutionary one. Jung built further upon this notion, positing the existence of a larger, numinous field of the unconsciousness that included archetypal, collective, and transpersonal dimensions. Following Jung, analysts such as Erich Neumann, James Hillman, Edward Edinger, Donald Kalsched, James Hollis, and Lionel Corbett continued to map the territory of the human psyche that Jung expounded upon years before.

Current theorists, such as Stan Grof and Ken Wilber have continued to bring further intellectual understanding to the perennial knowledge of emergence and integration of expanded states of consciousness that has been intrinsic to mystical systems for millennia. More recently, blending neuroscience with classical psychoanalytic notions of primary and secondary processes, Robin Carhart-Harris has proposed a new, more objective way of thinking about awakening. Harris' *Entropic Brain Theory* and REBUS model (relaxed beliefs under psychedelics) offer a neuroscientific perspective on how, when the ego (secondary process) relaxes deeper, previously inhibited unconscious processes (primary process) are given space to emerge and assimilate into awareness, thus expanding consciousness.

Relaxing ego functions *in service* of awakening to and re-membering who we are, both personally and transpersonally, has generally been the "golden thread" underlying the expansion of consciousness from the beginning of time. Whether in psychotherapy, as we microdose emerging awareness and integration, or in psychedelic therapies, rituals, or initiations where we might macrodose connection to and assimilation of the unconscious depths, we are opening channels to re-membering what lies at the foundations of who we are and to the field of a greater Source of consciousness from which we are born. How we do this is an important aspect of various approaches that have entered the clinical arena in recent years. Energy work (Reiki), hypnotherapy, breathwork, meditation, yoga, psychedelic therapy, and quantum consciousness approaches have all added significantly to mainstream psychotherapeutic technologies.

More recently, culture also has been increasingly open to the very old view that, before we arrive in the human dimension, we choose the particulars of each incarnation and the vantage points of awareness we wish to refine. Without this critical lens, it is difficult to comprehend the nature and trajectory of the Soul's journey through human life. I would like to acknowledge psychologist Michael Newton (*Journey of Souls*), for his courageous work in renewing this perspective in modern clinical discourse.

Moreover, from 30,000 feet up, we can begin to see that we are living in a story that has two main universal arcs. The *path of descending*, or *leaving* the ground of Self (differentiation and *immersion*), is the first arc in which, through continued incarnation, we build a temporary landing pad of identity that we refer to as the ego-self. The *path of ascending*, or *returning* to the original ground of being (Self) from which we *emerged* (re-integration), comprises the second arc. The path of descending encompasses the spring and summer seasons, during which we establish our home base within the immanent dimension of human life; the path of ascending, generally the work of the fall and winter seasons, not only holds a potential for re-connection with the depths of who we are, but also offers a return to wholeness through greater understanding that *all* dimensions (world, body, mind, spirit) are reflections of the One source from which we come.

The first half of life involves the unfolding, the necessary differentiation and formation of the polarities of Ego and Self, *when one becomes two,* the duality that is our task to reconcile in the second half of life. The second half faces us with the "higher" developmental challenge involving the mysterious process of the reconciliation or "chymical marriage" of these opposites, or as Jung would say: "*when two become one.*" *We must understand that, within these processes of unfolding and differentiation, the Self is always seeking integration and wholeness of all parts of being. These ideas are the cornerstone of Jung's notion of individuation and Neumann's overarching perspective on the "General Plan"*[1] *of lifespan psychological development.*

By *immersing* ourselves within the matrix of the time-space dimension, our task is to fully engage this human journey as the *Soul's practicum* for consciously realizing and integrating into our vibrational field the more abstract universal knowledge that is available to us before we arrived on this earthly plane. It is also the task of the soul to *emerge* and awaken to who we are and to do the most difficult work of learning how to manifest the Light of being within the full continuum of the human experience. Within this alchemical process, we discover that it is both through individual and collective engagement with the human experience that we refine our most

---

[1] Shany, L., Neumann, E. (2025). *The Theory.* Chiron Publications.

foundational capacities, evolving these intrinsic qualities (i.e., love, power, wisdom, beauty, understanding, kindness, discernment) into their more mature expressions, and as the kabbalists say, "raising the holy sparks."

— Kenneth R. Lakritz, Ph.D.

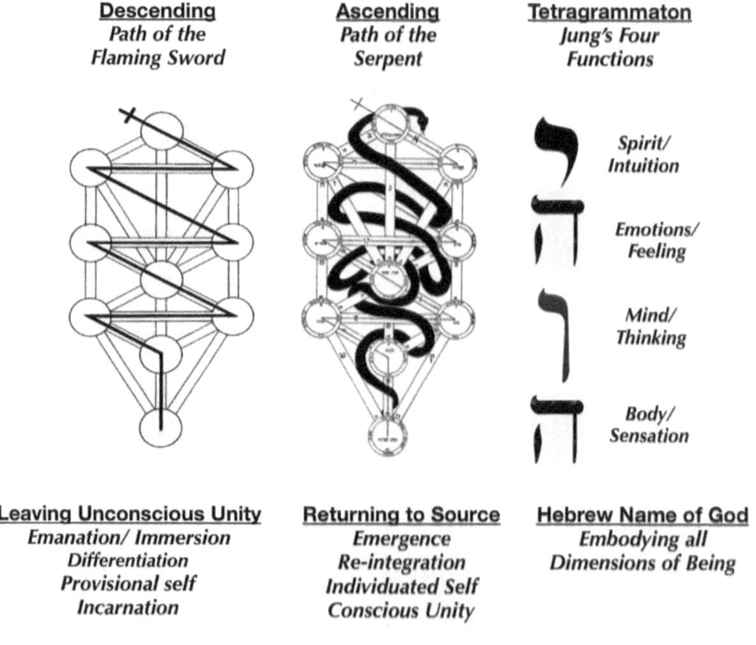

CHARACTERS

Shemah // Shemah is a 93-year-old elder, a fictional character, whose life story represents an aggregate of individuals whom Dr. Lakritz has encountered in his four decades of clinical practice. We witness the art of Self-discovery and the emergence of wisdom that consolidates with aging as Shemah engages the many-layered process of re-membering who he is.

Author // Dr. Lakritz, a clinical psychologist, is both facilitator and witness to Shemah as he reminisces upon his 93 years of living. Dr. Lakritz's presence may be viewed as a holding space for Shemah's reflections as he re-members his life both from a transcendent and personal perspective.

Cornelius // Cornelius' presence reflects the Soul guidance that lives within each individual. The mystery of his entrance into the process gradually reveals itself as Shemah awakens to the nature of his relationship with Cornelius. Through Cornelius, we are presented with a transcendent glimpse of the Soul's journey through the human experience.

How to read this book // This book is a window into death and dying, reminiscence and the reflections of aging, the process of reclaiming lost and segregated parts of the Self, and the universal threads that hold and reveal the Soul's deeper purpose.

As we accompany Shemah and Cornelius in a process of remembering, we are witness to reflections that hold both the larger, transcendent understanding of life's magnificence and the immanent, deeply personal experience of the travails of life as we navigate through the labyrinth of human existence. Cornelius, who enters Shemah's life as a child, mysteriously joins the Author and Shemah in the process of life reflection, providing a larger frame of reference for re-membering the Soul's intentions.

Beginning in present day, the book goes back in time to each season of life, presenting events that had become catalysts for Shemah's Soul journey. Following Shemah and Cornelius from Spring through Winter, a universal structure emerges for bringing into conscious awareness the threads of one's own veiled and challenging process of Self-realization. It is the hope of the Author that Shemah's recollections stimulate readers to reflect on seminal events in their own lives that have been transformational and opened "new," deeper landscapes of awareness.

Indeed, as you traverse through the labyrinth of life with the Author, Shemah, and Cornelius, you may very well find that you have taken many of the same turns and twists. As it is the journey of each Soul to tread the winding path back home, to re-member who you are, you may find yourself on common ground. In whatever season of re-membering you find yourself, may this book assist you in navigating your own Soul's journey and help to light the way as you walk toward a fuller awareness and expression of your true Self.

Ouroboros

We shall not cease from exploration
And the end of all our exploring
Will be to arrive where we started
And know the place for the first time

— T.S. Eliot

RE-MEMBERING

What Lives Within Us Longs to Be Remembered

The mythological theory of foreknowledge also explains the view that all knowing is "memory." Man's task in the world is to remember with his conscious mind what was knowledge before the advent of consciousness.
— Erich Neumann

When we enter the human body, we forget who we really are. To "forget" literally implies that there is something for us to get at some point in our journey through life. What is it that we must get that we have forgotten? What does it mean to re-member? Re-membering can be viewed as a process of re-collecting the experiences of a lifetime, like the weaving of patterns on a garment whose form, if we look closely enough, over time begins to coalesce into meaningful images. The heart of re-membering involves age-old, sacred practices that call each of us not only to examine the deeper meaning of our lives and suffering so that it may become more endurable, more livable, but also to make contact with the evolving story that lives within us. Re-membering also entails uniting those abandoned, forgotten, and exiled elements of our experience whose segregation from our hearts can create intense suffering and ultimately estrange us from ourselves. As we unfold with the seasons of life (see image at the end of this chapter), the process of re-membering makes possible a deeper contact with Self that allows us to re-call our original nature and, eventually, re-discover the foundation of who we really are. These emerging encounters with Self always come at a price, however. Carl Jung once said that encounters with the Self are often experienced as "defeat" by the ego.

I have long been contemplating the process of the unfolding of the human lifespan from the psychological, social, and spiritual perspectives. The recovery of larger memory begs the question of why we forgo awareness of our spiritual origins when we arrive in this human experience, and how it serves the soul that re-collection of our true nature remains unconscious and inaccessible throughout most of the first half of life? The question also remains as to whether earlier awareness of our higher intentions would help or hinder our engagement in the process of development and Self discovery as we move across the seasons? The mystery and meaning of the soul's journey throughout the changing landscapes of human life is largely what continues to draw me to these questions, and it is the privilege of participating intimately in the lives of my patients that calls me to take part in the unique process of each individual story. It was within the experiences of one of these individuals that I would get an opportunity to glean what I have been searching, consciously and unconsciously, for the greater part of my life.

It was an auspicious day when I met an elderly man named Shemah, who was called to my attention while I was working as a clinical psychologist in a skilled nursing facility. Many who have worked within or visited facilities like this know that they can be like warehouses for our old and infirmed, who are disengaging from life and simply waiting to die. Like others whom I had seen that day, Shemah also was preparing for, and contemplating, his own death. Unlike others, however, who were reflecting on days gone by with little more to live for, Shemah was engaged in a wholly different process that was leading him to consciously explore beyond the veil that divides life from death. He spoke to me of his daily journeys to the "other side," as he referred to it, where he would engage with other souls in what he described as both a briefing and de-briefing process. I was very intrigued by his notion of the other side and asked him if he would tell me more about what he was experiencing and learning from these travels. Before he died, we sat for weeks discussing his excursions to the "other side," his discoveries of the purpose and process of life's unfolding, and his reflections of a long journey lived to completion.

It was a brisk, clear fall afternoon when Shemah and I first spoke. I was performing my rounds and checking in with those individuals brought to my attention either by psychiatric difficulties or those able and interested enough to reflect on the meaning and closure of their lives. Shemah was unusual, however. Although he was a thin, frail-looking man in his nineties, he had the eyes of a child and a smile so warm that it penetrated deeply into the Souls of all who met him. He was filled with the happiness that clearly only comes from a sense of resolve and appreciation of a life fully lived. It was his joy that drew me into his story, and it was his wisdom that held me there. Entranced by the depth and breadth of his tale, I followed him through a many layered and multifaceted journey that reflected a life engaged with a sense of purpose and awe for the inner and outer workings of existence.

Clearly on the precipice, the veil that separates life from death was becoming thinner and more transparent for Shemah. Whether they were dreams, as he moved in and out of his frequent soporific moments, or whether they reflected lucid travels through subtle realms of consciousness that were now opening in ways that invited his presence, he was finding himself in between the life he knew and the larger sense of existence he was remembering. It was as if he had already experienced death and would continue to return to tell the tale as he remembered life from the point of view of one who can, again, see the larger, universal structure as it is meant to unfold. During our conversations, I began to realize that my presence, my witnessing, held an important holding space for his process as he reassembled the pieces of his life into a coherent pattern.

Being a psychologist for many years, I have often been witness to the process of remembering that allows others to integrate forgotten, or previously unconscious, material.

But this was different. Shemah's process of remembering appeared to extend to a level of recollection that seemed to go beyond the parameters of usual human awareness, to make contact with experiences that would normally be ascribed to the realm of mystics.

The framework of life that unfolded before us was profound and poetic. It was as if Shemah became a conduit for information usually only available to those in the process of crossing over. His ability to articulate what he was experiencing enabled him to re-member and metabolize his life in such a way that, when he finally released himself from his physical body, it was as if he had laid down a new strand of DNA in the helix that represented the experiences of many lifetimes. This gave me new insight into the reveries of aging, and the necessity of engaging seriously in the narratives of our own lives so that we, too, may carry within us the full extent of our experiences as we travel through the seasons (see image at the end of this chapter). I also realized that, before we transition from this level of being, we have a need to pass down the wisdom gleaned from a long life of incubated experience. I share this discourse not only to help us appreciate the sacred process of re-membering, but because I think that Shemah's story reflects something in the collective psyche that is hungry to remember its own purpose and re-invigorate its passion to participate in the profound mystery of human life.

The story told here of Shemah's journey through the lifespan is essentially a tale about an individual's dynamic, conscious evolution-awakening to the nature of being and creation. Shemah helped me to understand that how we experience our unique Essence, and channel the energies that flow from it, depends on the development and maturity of the vessel of self that contains and organizes its processes. He educated me that we often experience the Essence and its Container as different aspects of Being: the One "above," the One that is non-physical, transpersonal, and appears to us in universal images, and the One "below," the One that is experienced as physical, historical, personal and exists within the human condition. All mystical perspectives, he pointed out, indicate that these discrete facets of Being are a differentiated reflection of the One Source. Nonetheless, in our human lives, we tend to perceive these aspects dualistically and as distinctly different in how we understand them, talk about them, and experience them. The *transcendent* aspect, existing beyond space-time, appears to us to reflect something more ineffable, universal, and collective, while the *immanent* aspect, existing within space-time, appears to represent to us something more tangible, deeply personal, and uniquely individual. Yet, each level of being serves an irreducibly essential function in the alchemy of the consciousness we come to human life to evolve.

It is from this level of consideration that Shemah's story began to unfold between us. My usual work as a clinical psychologist tended to operate based on scientifically derived, evidence-based practices. The very organic and mystical nature by which this story unfolded between us represented a departure from my professional training and usual clinical practice. Something extraordinary and unusual occurred for me during my visits with Shemah, experiences that altered my whole view of life and how I conceived of my work as a clinical practitioner. My intrigue with the world view that was being disclosed before me allowed me to suspend disbelief in such a way that I could begin to glimpse the elegance and coherence of the wisdom that was being transmitted to me.

Through our dialogues, I was able to glimpse the memory of why we come to be in this human form and how we become able to discern and deepen our psychological and spiritual development. I witnessed in Shemah qualities that are essential to engaging the process of re-membering as a sacred art. It is simply not enough, I learned, to reminisce or recall the memories of our lives; sacred re-membering requires the capacity to listen deeply and to learn to understand the many levels and languages of the Soul. It also requires a courageous, open-hearted receptivity that enables us to embrace those isolated or rejected parts of ourselves that long to be held in the presence of love and compassion. Shemah's navigation of the labyrinth of living memory also exemplified the wisdom that is required to discern productive pathways and portals from those that are diversions, dead-ends, and traps. I came to see that it is usually those territories of self we most fear, where our alienation and suffering are pervasive, that call to us in numerous ways to engage in the process of re-membering.

Our interactions would often take unexpected but fertile directions as Shemah returned from across the threshold of his daily journeys to the other side. He would arrive from his expeditions with remarkable insights into the unfolding of human consciousness from the standpoint of one no longer tethered to the physical body. My curiosity about the juxtaposition of these transcendent insights with more immediate human experiences of life's unfolding led me to inquire more deeply about his own, more personal reflections of his journey from birth to old age. As we traversed the seasons from spring to the wintertime of life (see image at the end of this chapter), the sharing of both transcendent and immanent points of view allowed us to look at life, at being, through different, distinct lenses. I repeatedly found myself drawn to the perspective that reminds us that, for us to be as One, we must hold within the scope of our awareness multiple dimensions of being. During our talks together, we sought to hold the tension of these different levels of life's experiences, somehow knowing that appreciation of each vantage point would lead us to a deeper understanding of the human struggle.

I learned from Shemah that, as human beings, we are each on a quest to grow or expand by refining qualities that can only evolve from certain, chosen life experiences. These experiences enable the deepening of awareness and the development of our eternal capacities. Shemah understood, however, that *life must be lived through*, and not just comprehended. To live our quest, he felt, we must ultimately be present to both the joys and suffering of our human lives, embracing our finite state as if it were our eternal state of being. Herein lays the task for us all. He believed that because eternal and finite states are experienced as distinctly different, we fail to recognize that they are dual aspects of the same source of life. It is so challenging, he would say, to hold these polarities in consciousness without closing down the love that shines through when we are able to maintain an open-hearted presence to these opposites, especially when they embody both the good and the evil that lives within all human beings. He realized that we come late to a fuller appreciation of the permanence that underlies the impermanence of life. Fear and doubt, often pervading the greater part of our lives, hinder an open presence to our eternal core of Being. Without this receptivity, we cannot experience the depth of love and compassion that is the truth of who we are.

Shemah also conveyed that the space-time dimension provides an "outer" objectification of the "inner" subjective state. He offered:

This allows us the opportunity to be, at the same time, both the observer and the observed. Sense and emotion amplify subtle aspects of who we are so that they can be experienced and witnessed in tangible ways. The illumination of our inner experience also enables the refinement of awareness, making it possible to know more fully that which already exists within us in an undifferentiated state. Furthermore, the physical medium, like a hologram, manifests observable and measurable qualities that make the less palpable, energetic dimensions accessible to *conscious* discovery and discernment. This exteriorization of the interior world acts like a mirror that is continually feeding back to us information about our inner dynamics and processes. If we are mindfully listening and thoughtfully responding to the information that is continually reflected back to us and surfacing from deeper layers of the psyche, the human experience offers a unique opportunity for the evolution and refinement of our highest creative capacities.

The process of re-membering informs us that, when entering life, we do not enter with specific instructions. Our original intentions are soon forgotten shortly after birth until we slowly awaken during the course of the lifespan. While many of the circumstances within which we find ourselves are laid down before our physical birth, we must become conscious and intentful participants if we are to co-create with discernment as the mystery of our lives unfolds. As we awaken, we gradually remember that we did not come to be passive observers of a plan and a pathway fully determined for us before we entered human life. We receive that we are responsible agents, each of us playing a primary role in shaping the ways in which our lives manifest. As we re-member, we continually recognize the call to join thoughtfully in the creative dance that has always existed on all levels of being. The dance of life has always been one of active partnership in a progressively evolving emergence of Being that brings us closer and closer to a realization of conscious unity, of consciousness being fully conscious of itself.

THE FOUR SEASONAL PLATFORMS

SPRING

- *First birth* - leaving and differentiation from unconscious, undifferentiated Unity
- *Attachment / bonding* with primary caregivers
- Development of a *conditioned, provisional-biographical identity*
- Development of a *stable Ego complex* as center of consciousness and identity
- Establishment of a *family ground* as the First Platform
- Entering and becoming a member of the human community
- *Awareness of deeper Self remains dormant*
- Regulation of the life force energy is externally directed and perceived as originating from outside of self

---

SUMMER

- *First adulthood*
- Beginning of separation, *differentiation from family ground*
- Increasingly *independent regulation* of life force energy - still perceived as other or outside of self
- The Source of Love is perceived as originating primarily from others
- Immersed in the *immanent dimension* of human existence
- Identified with physical body and biographical identity
- Pursuit of relationships and work based on patterns of conditioning established in Spring

---

FALL

- *Second adulthood*
- *Differentiation of conditioned and unconditioned s / Self* begins
- Experience of death and mortification of identification with Ego
- Dark night of Soul - *Second birth* - involving reorganization of consciousness center as Self becomes emergent
- Encounter with Shadow and beginning *re - integration of dis - membered parts of self*
- Potential for Re-centering of consciousness in *immanent level of larger Self*
- *Centroversion - Awakening* of conscious link to the Eternal dimension of Being
- Beginning to perceive Source of Love as originating from *imperishable Self* / experienced as inside
- Potential for *conscious regulation* of and *co-creation* with life force energy

---

WINTER

- *Return to the Source of Being* begins
- Differentiation ends; *re - integration and emergence* continues
- Crossroad: attachment to / or differentiation from pre - midlife identification with body and conditioned identity
- *Preparing for death* and *third re - birth* and release from corporal form / identity begins
- Potential *harmonization of imminent and transcendent* dimensions of Being
- Potential *conscious re - integration* of all dimensions of being
- Possible *conscious linking with transcendent* dimension of Self - expands presence and capacity for compassion
- *Attachment to conditioned identity and body is released* as alignment with Unconditioned Being becomes increasingly crystallized
- Realization and *remembrance that we are facets of the life force energy* that we have perceived as other or outside of self in Spring and Summer

---

Modern thinking has often lost its way by separating the problem of truth from the problem of living, cognition from the total human situation... Reflection alone will not procure self-understanding. The human situation is disclosed in the thick of living.

— Abraham Joshua Heschel

PRECIPICE

The decisive question for man is: Is he related to something infinite or not?
— C.G. Jung

Shemah (1935)

I was eight years old when we first met. It was 1935, the height of the depression. It was early Saturday morning, the spring sunlight sliding through the window where my father sat with eyes closed and hands clasped over a stone mug of coffee. It was not unusual for him to take the silent, solitary pauses before others awoke. Always curious about these moments, I peered at his pensive brow from the threshold, watching him breathe, his chest the only thing the rising and falling to challenge the stillness. Shuffling into the corner of the room, I breached some unseen barrier, his one eye lifting to weigh my presence. His voice sounded full across the empty kitchen "Come here. Sit with me, son. Maybe it's time to share something." With his hand gently relaxing on my shoulder, he softly said, "Close your eyes, quiet your thoughts, and notice what emerges in the silence." I trusted my father, and sat soundless beside him, excited to find out what would happen.

Sitting for what felt like an ice age, my thoughts ran awry with what might arise. Suddenly, in my mind's eye, the image of a bearded elder came *forward with flowing gray hair and long, furry sideburns. He was wearing clothing from another time and place, a colorful silk, gray embroidered jacket, and a ruffled white ribbon tied around his neck. He seemed familiar in an odd way like an old friend or trusted advisor whom I had known for a very long time. I immediately slipped into the comfort of his presence like slipping on a well-worn ball cap, the fit of it curved to my head like a second skin. My mind flashed: Was he an angel? Was I making him up? Wisdom beaming through knowing eyes and a loving smile, he whispered, "I am Cornelius." With those words uttered into the hush, my mind recognized what my heart had been pulsing since I glimpsed his sage face: Cornelius was here for me, and me alone, and, somehow, we were eternally bound in a way I had yet to comprehend.*

The mystery that began with this auspicious morning visitation progressed to become one of the most important relationships of my life. When I was eight, I could not anticipate the integral role Cornelius would play in my life, nor fathom the depth of love and guidance that would always be there to sustain me. Similarly, I could not fully comprehend how the relationship would evolve or how the resulting transfigurations would define my connection with Cornelius as I entered later life. Yet at even the earliest blush, he was more than a guide or an inner archetypal image. He was a sustaining presence who nourished and filled me with a knowing that was beyond a mere eight-year-old boy just venturing into the world of humans. Looking back, this gift from my father, the passing on of the knowledge of inner life, the profound connection with an ineffable reality, was the bond that we shared until he died when I was 40.

It was the twilight of Shemah's 93rd year. He had been struggling with his health for some time, his attachment to life becoming so increasingly fragile that he labored to remain present to even the closest of those around him. "How fortunate," he said, "I am to be surrounded by such love: my wife, my children, my grandchildren, and the few friends who remain. As loved ones have passed to the other side, I have felt a growing connection to the unknowable, to the ethereal voices that whisper increasingly to me from beyond the veil that separates us from eternity."

Shemah continued:

My friends call me Shemah, which means "listen deeply." They gave me this name because listening is both my greatest gift and my deepest challenge. In recent years, I have been searching my memory closely for patterns that reflect something distinct about how consciousness, how the soul, evolves within the course of the lifespan. The human journey and its unfolding have often confounded me and, yet, have also inspired a deep sense of wonder for what is certainly the most magnificent of undertakings.

As I have reflected on my life, I have often thought how ordinary and how extraordinary we all are, many of us unable to find our greatness, our freedom in the sweetness of our true simplicity. It has taken a lifetime for me to see myself, to come to know myself in this mystery of being nothing and being everything, and to learn to harmonize the seeming contradictions and polarities of life. We all struggle with the tension of our differences, as well as with finding affirmation for the uniqueness of our distinct perspectives. Somehow, we still discover ways to maintain connection with one another while attempting to endure the loneliness of our solitary paths.

I am often overcome by the depth and miracle of our journey through life — the triumphs, the losses, the deepening spirals of self-awareness, the loving exchanges, and the shared joy of our human pilgrimage. All that's left for me now is the memory of love, for those moments of hearts touching in the fires of life's passions and challenges — brothers, sisters, mothers, fathers, sons, daughters, friends, and passersby. I take you all into myself. I am so grateful for all of it, for all of you. I will remember you in the vibrating strings of my soul. I know now that all that we feel and all that we touch is drawn into the core of being, each a part of the personal, cosmic memory — the Essence that remains after all else dissipates.

Each day, I have been feeling that I am at the precipice of death, experiencing my death over and over as if in a dream. I find that there is a strange alchemy that presses upon the spirit when we slowly become entombed in a dying body that restricts our natural fluidity. The muting of physical processes as we die appears to release us from the debris of thoughts and feelings no longer consequential to the fading mind. As I dream of my death, I see that Essence, only Essence remains. How long I have strived for this quality in life, only to be captured over and over in the flypaper of my biological hardwiring and psychological conditioning. I have lived my life as but a poor imitation of what I feel myself becoming in death, finally myself, finally the one I have sensed in the deepest, silent moments. As I experience myself at death's doorstep, awareness rises that we are not lost in death but rather, finally, again found.

In my dreams, I see this mirrored in the faces of my loved ones, knowing that it is the gift that I leave, my legacy realized in the final moments of my passing. I found myself experiencing both the tears and joy of my final seconds, my heart bursting open as the body mortifies, my spirit pushing out as if through some ethereal birth canal. My kiss, my departing embrace, pouring out a lifetime of love and appreciation through the countenance of my last breath. I felt released. I said to myself, "I am coming home."

I dreamed that I had died. What a wonderfully expansive feeling to peel away from the physical body! It is like shedding an old skin or outgrowing a once-loved pair of shoes. It's like the peace one feels of the calm after a ravenous storm. The freshness, the color I felt in an absence of pain. It has seemed like a very long time since I have been without pain in my body as well as my heart. I felt as though released from a shell separating my heart and my mind from the source of all being. I felt whole again, complete. I said to myself, "Yes, I am remembering!"

I always thought that I would be greeted by loved ones — my parents, grandparents, old friends — but instead found myself waiting in something like a room with other beings who were unfamiliar to me. They appeared to have anticipated my arrival and were eager to converse with those who continue to carry the resonance and memory of human life's unfolding from birth to old age. They were also in transition, soon to engage the cycle of birth and the vicissitudes of human life and death. In my dream, I became aware that it is customary here to share in the reflections of a newly departed life before the felt memory falls away. Words, I found, were no longer the medium for communication. Thoughts, feelings, and images were conveyed directly as if we were all just different facets of one consciousness, each with our distinct perspective but no longer separate. We were all emanating from and flowing into one Source. Strangely, we were all One, and yet never did I ever feel more myself.

There were eight other beings present with me within this space that I am conceiving of as a room, even though it was clear to me that we relinquish space-time when we emancipate from the shell of the physical. The opportunity to debrief with others of our human journey appeared to be a great gift that allows us to complete the assimilation of thoughts, feelings, and experiences that have gestated over a lifetime. The telling of the story of a human life is deeply meaningful here, not because we may call upon it as a resource while in the tumults of existence, but because it reminds us of the nobility, the joys, and the fruits of the venture into the world of matter.

To my great surprise and delight was the presence of a dear old friend that I had known since childhood, Cornelius, who was here to preside over this assembly of souls in the sacred capacity of the "Overseer." An Overseer is present at each soul's transition and functions to help bring form to the seemingly unrelated pieces or threads of an individual life. Cornelius' role was to assist me in the consolidation of those living images, experiences, and memories I had gathered like precious stones from a lifetime in the human body. The ones who offer themselves to this important task are here to remind us that there is a known, predictable structure to the unfolding of consciousness while traveling in the vehicle of the physical body. There are multiple levels of debriefing, and each level is to be communicated simultaneously to help weave together the garment of the newly departed life so that it may seamlessly enter the larger fabric of being.

I remember Cornelius stating that, as beings travel in and out of the physical dimension, it is a natural tendency to search to connect with the memory and meaning of what often becomes lost during the voyage through life. He said, "While in the thick of human existence it is very easy for us to forget why we enter and how we grow individually and as a whole from our explorations within physical creation. The challenge is to remain as awake as possible to the transcendent currents of our deeper intentions while we move through the dense, heavy gravitational forces intrinsic to human life." Cornelius continued:

As expressions of one source, we each reflect distinct qualities and perspectives of the whole of Being. At our core, we are adventurous and joyous and drawn to new vantage points from which to focus our creative energies. The great value that we place on the development of each of our evolving capacities inspires us to explore a variety of media. Ventures within a never-ending multitude of possible ways of engaging our expansion allow us to deepen awareness of the many available dimensions of thought and feeling. The dense vibrational substrates of physical resonance are one such pathway within which we seek these experiences, and from which we strive to awaken new, yet unknown, avenues of consciousness.

Human existence, as we have come to know it, has not always been available for our creative expression and expansion. There are many other such media from which to express our intentions, and from which to develop our unique qualities and potentialities. When we chose to explore the space-time matrix, we discovered a novel substrate for forming and focusing our energies. The precise alchemy generated between the polarities of so-called "physical" and "non-physical" states enables possibilities for awakening consciousness unlike anything that exists. Unique properties of this medium make possible a gradual, organic unfolding of life that allows for the reflection on our choices and intentions. Thoughts and feelings also manifest in more explicit ways than on more subtle energetic levels, and like a sculptor modeling clay, we are given space-and-time to fashion and refine our creative vision. As life unfolds, we witness that the rough grains of physical resonance permanently etch and contour the ever-evolving formation of our being the way glaciers chisel the mountains and valleys. As artists, one may have the tools for creating a work, but without the felt, lived experience and evolving depth of perspective, the forms generated will lack texture and dimension.

The temporal medium has developed in ways that provide an unlimited diversity of sensory forms (visual, sound, taste, touch, etc.), emotions, ideas, and vantage points. Within these parameters, it is as if we are presented with an infinite array of possible ways of looking at self and life, and from which we may experience inexhaustible opportunities for new perspective. It is the ongoing tension of ever differing, contrasting, and conflicting viewpoints that makes possible the refinement of the focus of our intentions. The soil and climate within which we choose to plant our lives (i.e., our physical bodies, families, cultures, geographic locations, and temporal circumstances) provide the platform for specific trajectories that set into motion the unfolding of physical capacities, awareness, and creative opportunities. Both the journey and the destination of our chosen lives bring clarity to the awareness we come to gather and enlarge our appreciation of the boundless possibilities extant within the human experience.

The rich soil from which we spring provides the ground and direction of our lives and the path that unfolds from it. There is no end to the panorama of perspectives that we may cultivate as we evolve, and it is the joy of awareness and evolution that continues to attract us to enter this dimension. Yet, as we traverse the peaks and valleys, we also understand that light may be accompanied by equal degrees of darkness as we fully engage in the tasks and cycles of the human journey. Before we plant the seed of our being within the physical organism, we are clear that it is within these embodied circumstances that we add depth and texture of felt experience to the tools of our creative armamentarium.

A great poet once said, "If you have not experienced it, it isn't true."[2] This is the universal foundation of all evolution of consciousness. We cannot paint a landscape with only a limited array of colors, hues, and textures. To refine our creations, we must have at our disposal an ever-expanding range of the universal qualities incubated and matured from lifetimes of concentrated development. From our larger frame of reference, however, to effectively utilize these instruments of intentionality, we must be well-acquainted with their resonance and potential for actualization. We have learned from our many travels that resonance experienced through sense, emotion, and cognition allows for fully integrated awareness of it. This provides a relationship with the vibrating elements of the universe that is not abstract but lived. Fully lived experience gives breadth, color, dimension, and feeling to the forms we generate; it also evolves these qualities from unconscious, undifferentiated forms to conscious, increasingly articulated ones that can be used with greater precision.

---

[2] Kabir (2004). *Kabir: Ecstatic Poems* (R. Bly, Trans.). Beacon Press.

Listening to Cornelius, I was reminded of why I chose to engage, to breathe in the dense, beautiful, and oftentimes noxious elements of human existence. I remembered that the flowers of awareness blossom most fruitfully when immersed in the fertile soil of the physical dimension. Nonetheless, I have often found that when touched by the oftentimes overpowering energies coursing through the body, captive to the formidable grip of psychological and social forces, I no longer felt as if I held the artist's brush of my own destiny. These heavy constraints often left me feeling as if I had put my head inside a tiger's mouth from which there was no bargaining for release. Ambivalent, reluctant, and stumbling forward, I frequently lost my bearings within my own confusion about what chosen purpose lay before me in my ever-unfolding but finite path through the human world. I often struggled to find direction and meaning within the complex, intricately interwoven fabric of daily existence, and I found myself recoiling time and again from the very life that I entered with such enthusiasm and determination.

It was not until the latter part of my life that I began to understand the patterns fundamental to the cycles of human development and to experience the intrinsic worth of my deepest suffering. I became aware of how I often squandered precious energies in efforts to avoid immersion into the very experiences I came to gather. My life, like that of many others, was an imperfect balance of strivings, of attempts to give and receive and to cope with the ever-shifting landscape and weight of my evolving journey. I came to realize that I often attempted to bypass the inherent dualities of life without understanding that I chose this journey because of the way that its polarities (good and evil, ego and Self, eternal and finite, etc.) teach us about unconditional love.

Mindful of the back and forth of my dialogue with Cornelius, I began to understand the importance of debriefing in this fashion. I noticed a dance of fluctuating levels of awareness as I conveyed my fresh, human experience against the backdrop of the more universal structure articulated by Cornelius. Together, we were holding the felt experience of human life in a way that honored its unique qualities, its wholeness, and its complexities within a context that gives meaning and universality to what seemed, otherwise, to be random and without purpose.

Here is more of what Cornelius told me: "Because we are eternal, we are always seeking to enlarge our awareness in ways that reflect a fully integrated, lived-experience of it. Before we enter the physical dimension, we choose life circumstances that will enable us to develop and refine specific qualities we wish to include in the DNA of our being. From the human standpoint, it is impossible to comprehend why particular conditions are chosen. The narrow view of human consciousness limits our ability to remember and grasp the origins of intentionality from which we choose experiences that may broaden our vibrational repertoire. It is often not until the end of life that the patterns of our unique evolution are revealed in ways that can bring greater understanding of the meaning of the paths chosen."

Responding to Cornelius' message, I found myself very moved by the choices made as a basis for our individual human experiences. It was clear to me that no other can even begin to appreciate the context from which a life is decided. One here will enter a village in Africa, ravaged by war and famine, only to die at a very tender age from starvation. Another will enter a body disfigured by genetic abnormality, plagued by multiple surgeries and chronic physical and emotional suffering. Another will live an extremely affluent and privileged life but will live through the challenges of chemical addiction and crippling emotional isolation. Yet another will have early emotional trauma so severe that he will spend much of his life in and out of institutions fighting each day for his very sanity. Humanity will watch helplessly while ethnic groups are cleansed in mass genocide, or as others are killed for the color of their skin or the content of their beliefs. Within all this suffering, however, I could see that we are also witness to the great joys of the heart and the miraculous courage and tenacity of the spirit. We clearly learn that, by living within and through the challenging and painful circumstances of human life, our creative energies can and do thrive, and we are able to affirm and awaken what is most deep and true in our being. Then Cornelius spoke again:

> The circumstances we choose for our lives continually give us guidance to grow in new and more conscious directions. These conditions, while often a pervasive source of conflict and suffering, operate as an inner Guru (teacher that brings light from darkness) that serves to unlock awareness that would otherwise remain dormant, underdeveloped, and undifferentiated. We might experience this inner "Guru" as an inescapable wound or a daimonic energy that we feel compelled to heal or excise. It often takes a lifetime to come to an appreciation of the transformative potential that these circumstances provide as they act upon consciousness and call us to awaken our interior depths. This inner Teacher is the gift and the challenge that we offer ourselves so that we will not be able to bypass or turn away from the sacred tasks of each of our unique journeys. It cannot be exorcised, removed, or healed; it is our blessing and our burden, and the primary vehicle of our expansion.
>
> Before we take residence in human life, it is an accepted understanding that awareness or memory of our origins becomes dormant during predictable periods of early

development. While this dimension is highly valued for its transformative properties, long periods of maturation are required for the human organism to make a healthy adaptation to survive the intensive demands of biological and social conditions. For the first half of life, we must concentrate the majority of our energies to this end. This must be so for us to develop the skills and capacities needed to navigate and create while in this state of Being.

During the dormancy period of the Self, we form bonds or alignments with those specifically chosen by us before birth. These are individuals on whom we depend for the purposes of our very survival. We look to these souls for their care and guidance, because, instinctively, we know that we have yet to develop the abilities necessary to independently navigate this new ground of existence. We naturally entrust our souls to our mothers, fathers, teachers, and elders so that they may help maintain a needed connection for us with the original foundation of all Being, a state which is natural for us before we enter the human body. We innately "know" that in the absence of either direct or indirect connection with our origins, we will be unable to thrive in this new form, and the processes and challenges of being human will exceed our ability to cope.

This fundamental relationship between older and younger pilgrims is integral to the evolution of human consciousness. An intentful bond between generations makes possible the healthy facilitation of a Soul's transition from one developmental life period to another. Properly supported transitions enable a gradual shifting of self-identification that can open doorways to our fuller creative capacities. Immersed within a very challenging biological and psychological environment, however, we must first begin with the necessary formation of a *preliminary* identity that is adaptive to the demands of early development. This provisional, biographical self is critical for navigating very complex biological, psychological, and social dimensions of human existence. After these capacities are well-established within the context of the life structure, we will be better able to attune ourselves to the presence of both inner and outer signs that progressively call us to explore new layers of being. If we are receptive to the loving guidance of elder pilgrims who have achieved fuller awareness of who they are, we may be enabled in the process of re-membering our own Essential roots.

Human evolution, unfortunately, has seen a structural collapse of the roles elder pilgrims play in properly fostering these important developmental crossings. The loss of the conscious inter-connection between those in each season of life weakens the potential for our evolution. The transition period from dormancy of awareness to one of conscious relationship with the Source of all life does not progress in the absence of *mature* midwives who can help to birth us into new, expanded levels.

Without a felt sense of meaning regarding our original intentions, we are susceptible to aborting our journeys or becoming overtaken by the very powerful influences of our primitive, biological hardwiring. Lack of connection to the truth of who we are and why we are here leaves us subject to the long-evolved, instinctual impulses of the organism in which we now reside. Prolonged alienation from the core of being can produce suffering so intense as to fuel violence toward others or provoke premature decisions to abandon the lives we entered with such intentionality. When we journey through life, we are not meant to be isolated from the Essence of who we are. There are many stories and resources created by pilgrims of past incarnations whose availability can help give us perspective regarding distressing experiences that may leave us feeling deeply wounded and perplexed about the meaning of our presence in this dimension.

We are not able to make sufficient sense of our experiences without either direct inner alignment with the memory of who we are or close connection with someone who has become a living conduit for us, one who can help us to see ourselves through the wise eyes of an evolved other. An absence of connection with our authentic core can cause us to feel at odds with our chosen lives, or to feel as if forsaken and fundamentally alienated from the source of love from which we originate. Loss of understanding about why we enter is a known consequence of the broken link between young human beings and older ones; elder pilgrims are meant to light and lighten our way as we heroically engage the path of Self-discovery. It is this gradual awakening that calls many elders to offer guiding hands to younger ones, who they know are so vulnerable to losing their way in the great ocean of life's seductions and illusions.

Shemah found himself responding with these words, "In the latter years of my life, I began to feel intentful hands reaching across the veil to those of us who were receptive to a renewal of connection. In much the same way that elders and mentors had reached out to me during my youth, I discovered that those who had passed earlier were extending loving hands to me again, offering a connection between worlds whose continuity I had often questioned. I began to understand that the cycles of life are not broken when we transform from one form or state into another; those of us who have engaged the next levels of being are most able to light the pathway for those souls struggling to find the doorway through which some of us were already humbly able to pass. Without loving guidance from elder pilgrims, I know that I might never have found passage through this very subtle, inner portal which I have worked diligently to maintain as a beacon for others who were interested in making the journey."

Cornelius then explained, "From our many excursions, we have learned that souls passing to and from this dimension benefit greatly from sharing with those recently immersed in the human experience. For a short time after a soul leaves the physical body, it continues to carry the living resonance that evolves from a lifetime within this level of existence. Communions of this kind allow those in transition to briefly brush against the dissipating field of consciousness before the skin of felt human memory sheds completely. They also help those who are returning home to consolidate memories from this long journey through the seasons of life."

Again, Shemah responded to Cornelius, "I am aware of the importance of this level of discourse as I begin to reflect on the patterns and cycles of the life with which I participated for so long. While the story of my passage through the seasons is a chronicle of my unique venture through the processes of Self-discovery, I can see that there are universal threads that run through everyone's evolving story. My greatest challenge was often to hold the unfathomable course of my life with appreciation for the mysterious ways in which the movements of the Soul entered and guided me. Meeting in this transitional place, I noticed that those who were soon to enter the dimension from which I was returning took pleasure in co-mingling with a still-vibrating field of human consciousness. In their presence, however, I was finding myself drawn in a different way, realizing that I was being pulled further and further beyond this known resonance to a medium I was only beginning to remember. It was this simultaneous blending and sharing of multiple levels that was bringing my lived experience into clearer focus, assisting me in gradually finding my way back to my original state."

Then Cornelius remarked, "No life can be fully understood or evaluated from its particulars. A wider lens is required to appreciate the whole of life from birth to death, as well as the transcendent threads that hold it together in a coherent pattern. While development often occurs in logical, sequential stages, non-linear, synchronistic, and mysterious patterns also weave through and shape life in ways that can only be apprehended when a larger field of awareness is brought into view. A harmony of both lived experience and a broader viewpoint is necessary to fully appreciate the patterns that emerge from the interwoven pieces of our lives. Human development may be viewed in terms of distinct seasons, not unlike those found within the natural biological world. Each season is unique in its experience and nature, and no life period, including the tasks that comprise it, is richer or more valuable than any other. All developmental phases are interdependent, requiring mutuality in establishing the seasonal platforms upon which each structure of life is built. The soil upon which we create is crucial to building the sub-structures that provide stepping-stones or bridges to new levels of awareness."

Shemah tried then to respond to what he had heard, "As I describe my journey, I will try to convey a broader sense of the patterns to which

I was witness, knowing that the garment that each of us weaves as we stitch together the pieces of our lives is personal and unique. In my visits to the other side, I remembered that there is a universal structure to the cycles of life. I recalled beginning with a sense of unity of which I was not yet conscious. I was initially dependent upon the love and care of more experienced pilgrims to guide me through the early phases of my maturation. With the compassionate aid of others, I was able to gather memories of my journey in a way that eventually enabled me to re-discover the larger dimensions of being from which I came. In time, I became one of those elder pilgrims who were able to gratefully give the food of essence to those new souls who were much in need of its sustenance. We play such important roles in helping one another achieve new plateaus from which to engage in life. Without connection to the Source that breathes meaning into the very difficult trials of human existence, I feel that we are like boats adrift on dark, stormy seas."

CORNELIUS' TEACHING

Out of suffering have emerged the strongest souls; The most massive characters are seared with scars.

— Kahlil Gibran

Remembering the first time we touched matter was like planting a seed in the richest of soils. We watched the seed take root and branch forward into an ever-expanding multiplicity, differentiating and recombining into new and beautiful forms, rhythmically flowering and shedding, eventually becoming something so much larger and magnificent than the character of its original essence. We saw ourselves as these seeds and were drawn to the possibilities, the energies, the consciousness that could be unlocked if we immersed ourselves in various conditions of human existence. From that beginning, journeys uniting the Essence of Being with the dense vibrational matrix of the physical dimension have deepened and refined our understanding of the way certain variations of biological, psychological, social, and spiritual conditions create platforms from which unique vantage points of consciousness may evolve. We found that it was through our continued incarnation within this level of existence that, as a collective, we were able to become conscious of that which lies at the deepest roots of being.

The alchemists of early humanity were known for their attempts to transform base metals, such as lead, into gold. Using specific elements, they were engaging in a process that is at the heart of all evolution within the universe. True alchemy was the mystery of unfolding, not just from the mixing of physical elements, but from the joining of our spiritual Essence with the conditions of experience within human life. From combining the source of life with the fertile soil of the physical body and environment, a growing, flowering being may evolve into ever differentiating forms. The gold we seek is not the metal the early alchemists were said to have sought, but the fruits of awareness, of perspective, of clarity, of inner harmony that are born and refined when the seed of our Original Being both deepens its roots and flourishes outward from its immersion in the fecund soil of human experience.

Regardless of our state of being, there is really no such thing as past or future. There is only that which resides eternally within the accumulated lived experiences of the Soul. The unique quality of human memory is that it provides us with temporal and spatial points of reference for entering and re-entering experiences that always live within us in the present. There are many doorways through which to enter our experiences; memory provides us with the working mechanism for chronicling and selectively searching the connections and various shared pathways of what comes to comprise who we are. Human beings are quite vulnerable, however, to splitting off and compartmentalizing experience in ways that preclude full metabolization or integration. The intensity of human emotion and the tendency to shy away from experiences too painful or unacceptable to face create pockets of stagnant energy that, if left unattended, fester and arrest the natural process of unfolding. It is a perennial and sacred art to know how to enter portals of memory in ways that assist with metabolization, and in ways that enable the alchemy of human experience to perform its job of transforming and releasing the energy of new consciousness.

We usually enter the process of re-membering through the vehicle of the story, and in particular, the story of a life. A personal narrative, with all its biographical and pre-biographical elements, is a living, breathing entity. Its evolution within us has a unique chemistry, with its own set of experiences and wounds, offering each of us a distinctive perspective of ourselves and the world. It is often our wounds, our symptoms, our personal and developmental challenges that call us to become more interested in our interior world and the creative process that is generated from the unique dynamics of our lives. The art of re-membering involves the capacity to enter the heat, the suffering that lives within the wounded places of the soul, so that split-off, abandoned, or avoided experiences can be re-collected and re-united with the whole of our being. Without the ability to embrace these areas of self-alienation, our energies languish and generate further, deepening suffering.

To go further into the memory of life, to uncover the depths of our origins, we must have both guidance and courage to face those hot places within our living story where the transformative energies are most fierce and potent. Without the active process of *presencing* our experiences of both joy and suffering, we cannot deepen awareness nor uncover our full creative potential. We must learn to be like fishermen, fishing for living images that lead to the portal of memories yet to be recollected. What lives inside us longs to be re-united in consciousness, in meaning, and it will call to us ever louder in the form of physical and emotional symptoms until we can eventually reclaim all that passes through our hearts. We must befriend our grief, for it is not a statement of letting go of what we love, but rather an emotional expression that involves embracing and honoring what something or someone has meant to us. A fuller experience of grief also welcomes awareness of even the most unimaginable experiences that might live in isolation from our hearts and separate us from ourselves.

We are ultimately not meant to live in separation from ourselves but may find that the unique circumstances of our lives require that we must learn to endure and survive in the harshest of environments. For awareness to manifest, we must often gestate in hostile surroundings, alienated and devoid of the love from which we originate. Until we can re-collect and embrace these memories, we will remain hostage to the experience of victimization, unable to generate the larger awareness for which we chose these sets of circumstances. As discussed, we all have "informed consent" as we make our way along the pathway of our chosen lives. Before we enter, we know just how hot and intense the fires are of lived, human experience. We know that we must learn to welcome and embrace our experiences for consciousness to transmute and expand. Yet, we forget just how easy it is to fall asleep to these realities, often living in mortal fear of the very task of re-membering that is most central to our journey. We tend to make so many conditions about what we wish to hold within our awareness that we miss or turn away from the very experiences we come to behold.

We might find ourselves feeling justified in turning away from the pain generated from perceived wounds, building a life and identity designed to avoid or soothe those unattended areas of experience which cause so much anguish. Our self-reinforced blindness makes it nearly impossible for us, alone, to enter those portals of memory in such a manner that enables the expanded consciousness that these pockets of suffering are meant to produce. The Soul does not tolerate separation well or for long, however. We come from Unity, and we hunger to be united within ourselves, suffering immeasurably when we feel unwelcome in our own bodies and lives. We are only able to turn away from our experiences for so long before they begin to generate illness. We may seek healing for the symptoms of our disturbance, or we may eventually begin to become curious about re-membering who we are and why we came to be in this life. Like a phone that never stops ringing, our lives will never stop calling us to remember.

Some of us choose lives that are filled with insurmountable pain and darkness, lives in which it is difficult to discover the beauty and miracle of human existence. Sometimes we choose these experiences to quicken our consciousness of human vulnerability and to begin to be able to perceive the subtleties in creation of which we would otherwise be unaware. Like the prodigal son, it is often the tension, the degree of separation from our origins, which provides the perspective needed to create a true awareness of who we are in our Oneness. When we sum up our lives, it will likely be the most challenging of circumstances that we re-call as our finest moments; it will be the difficult and anguishing choices that will remind us of our deepest values; and it will be the suffering most faced that will fill our hearts with the clarity and joy of awakening.

As we engage in the process of re-membering, we must learn that it will take great skill and time to differentiate our own story from those of others. There are as many stories as there are beings present. Throughout our lives, we will be vulnerable to confusing our own path with that of others. While there is so much that we must take in as our own during our early development, there is an equal amount that we must discard along the way to separate our own journeys from those of all others. Our early needs to feel secure and aligned with others draw us to seek a shared truth and view of reality, where, in fact, consensual reality is simply a human construction. We fear that relative truth and uniqueness of perspective will disrupt social order and break the threads that bind us to one another. In our discernment and discovery of our own uniquely evolving path, we will realize that the opposite is true. As we awaken to and embrace our destinies in all their elements, we will feel a deeper respect and appreciation for the unique and sacred journey of all others. In our re-membering, we will also recall that all being arises from One Source, inexorably and unbreakably tied as one family.

Whether in our awareness or not, our narratives and the resonance that reside within us pour into the world like an eternal fountain. This flow of consciousness shapes and contours our reality in ways that are first based upon the conditioning that pervades during early periods of life. Like a mirror, the story that inhabits our lives constructs the world of relationships and events that come to comprise our reality. To begin to understand what lives within, we need to look no further than the world around us that reflects that which resonates so powerfully from the depths of our hearts and minds. When we feel punished by any circumstances, look not for the perpetrator but for the beliefs that create the conditions in which we feel ourselves victimized. If we feel neglected or abandoned, look not at those who have left us behind but, rather, at the ways in which we have become unavailable to ourselves. When we see evil in the world, look not for the outer source of moral corruption but for the disowned parts of our inner life that we are projecting on to others. Properties of the physical dimension provide an exteriorization of the subjective world unlike any that exists in the universe. It concretely feeds back to us the ways in which the subtle and not so subtle influences of our living resonance shape our immediate world. Until we come to know our own inner landscape intimately and become aware of the specific ways we consciously and unconsciously project our inmost thoughts and feelings upon our outer environment, our life patterns will continue to repeat themselves over and over again.

Discernment is a subtle and sacred art, and one that often requires a wise companion assisting us with seeing that which might be invisible or too unbearable to experience alone. Resistance to looking into the mirror may inform us that a sacred container held by a skillful guide is necessary to help us explore those tender places where the heat of our inner life cannot be held in isolation. Within the labyrinth of living memory, there are many detours and dead ends that lead us astray from re-membering and re-aligning with who we are. In the absence of a trusted companion, we may be prone to reinforce those areas of blindness that shield us from experiencing our unknown, sacred depths. Re-membering requires courage and a willingness to feel the broken heartedness of life's imperfections, unmet needs, and expectations. It requires an openness that invites us to view our lives with sobriety and honesty, making possible an experience that honors the conditions in which all human beings find themselves. A willingness to be fully present to our stories, to re-member with clarity and compassion, will eventually open the gates of consciousness from which all creativity is born.

As we reach the end of our time, we may find ourselves re-assembling stray pieces of memory like the gathering of leaves in fall. The call of death is mobilizing and organizing and does not like to leave the garment of life unfinished. We may be surprised at the richness and coherency of the patterns that have coalesced from the seemingly meaningless, disconnected experiences of our journey. What was and was not completed in life, however, remains that which travels with us through the portal that transitions being from one state to the next. What resonates within us in life is carried with us in death. The garment we carry of our travels is not for us alone, however; it is shared joyously with the larger collective as it ever evolves and learns from our courageous endeavors. The art of creation is of the highest value for us, and to create with the utmost level of skill and intentionality, we must always hold as the central task to re-member who we are.

SPRING

The two most important days in your life are the day you are born and the day you find out why.

— Mark Twain

Shemah (1943)

*T*he Big War, WWII, took all of us captive. In a darkened movie house, freshly made popcorn saturated the air as we watched For Whom The Bell Tolls. During the double feature intermission, my eyes gaped in horror as I stared at news reels of emaciated and broken bodies, skin stretched over limbs, and heads piled in newly dug trenches. Crematoriums fumed beside murderous gas chambers. My stomach turned as I witnessed this uncensored inhumanity from the safety of my plush seat in the local theatre. I came excited to see the main feature, Heaven Can Wait with Gene Tierney, but was no longer able to concentrate after witnessing the atrocities unfolding overseas.

The following played on repeat in my thoughts: "How could the stories my parents told me about God be true? If there was such a God, how could he allow this?" I couldn't breathe. My mind swirled, suffocating as my childhood shattered against the stark black and white screen. "Heaven won't wait if *there isn't one." At that moment, my emerging sense of self felt stripped of any remaining remnants of naivety that cloistered me from the awareness of human evil. For me, as Nietzsche had remarked, "God was dead," and there was no resurrection in sight. I sat nauseous and silent as a numbing feeling spread across my body, anesthetizing my heart. I left the theatre, no longer a teenager, as unknown to myself as those inert corpses lumped into mass graves. There was no turning back.*

At home, the spiral continued. I pressed Cornelius into the innermost recesses of my mind, locking his penetrating gaze and infectious smile firmly in the hope chest of childhood memories alongside my Lone Ranger mask and the rest of the discarded toys.

Then came 1946. Sitting at my dimly lit college dorm-room desk, a radio played Benny Goodman's "I'm Just Dreamin'" softly, while I stared at the wall. Out the window, winter reappeared with returning GIs' somber eyes and sunken faces telling me nothing and everything of their hollowing experiences. I looked down at my hands, my arms, my legs — intact, but not anywhere whole. A sense of loneliness, helplessness, and guilt breached my awareness as I questioned the value of my life and, for the first time, contemplated if I should be here at all. These thoughts echoed through my body, trying to lodge, attach, embed. I could feel them digging, trying to gain purchase. Tugging at the corners of my heart, they tried to find soft spots between the folds to penetrate the center of my being. As I felt myself starting to entertain these emerging ruminations, a familiar presence intervened: "There will never again be another you!"

Listening intently, I wondered if I had heard those words at all. From somewhere, deep, and not nearly as muffled this time, it was repeated: "There will never again be another you!" Kind eyes and a gentle smile flashed as I remembered: Cornelius. As I said his name out loud into the quiet, breathing him into life within once more, I felt an opening, and a burgeoning choice, which I had not before been able to perceive. A landscape, blooming as large as the universe itself, projected before me, revealing my smallness in an expanse beyond comprehension, beyond earth, sky, and star. As I stood on the ledge before eternity, the limits of outer and inner vision receded. After another breath, the grand vision faded, and I fell back into life's gravity, chest constricting and heart squeezing under unbearable pressure that took the wind from my lungs. At the edge of the crush, however, I grasped for any source of light. In reaching, I felt hands begin to support me from within, steadying me, offering me leverage from the gyre into the abyss. In that instant, I knew that I was responsible for choosing to fall into the chasm, or to allow something deep within provide guidance and rescue. With all the courage I could muster, I answered Cornelius: "OK. I'm listening; show me the way through."

Spring // Author

As Shemah returned from each new excursion in his dreams and in his reflections, he was eager to share with me what he was remembering with the facilitation of the Overseer he referred to as Cornelius. He was often surprised at how easily we forget the most simple and obvious truths, and how they become buried by our emersion in everyday demands. This was the start of what became a long process that carried us from the beginning to the end of Shemah's life. Excited by the discourse of the debriefings with Cornelius, he was always very animated as he began to retell what was conveyed to him in this most sacred process of re-membering.

With each recounting of the Overseer's broader perspective of the unfolding of human life through the seasons, I encouraged Shemah to tell his story and to remember the meaningful moments of his own life. The blending of both universal and individual perspectives gave a glance at the different levels on which we experience the unfolding of the Soul's journey through the human lifespan. It was like looking at the same process from two uniquely different vantage points: one, a broader and more detached appreciation of the purpose and process of the journey, and the other, the lived human experience that plunges the person into the dense emotional and organic nature of life as it unfolds within us. It seems to be the human task to learn how to hold the tension between intellectual understanding and living-through.

As Shemah recounted Cornelius' words, it was as if he was transported into an altered state during which he became almost like a channel or an oracle, strangely able to bring words to a usually ineffable level of understanding. It was like being in a classroom on the way to, or from, another life, another incarnation, a stop along the way to consolidate memories from a long life or to prepare for re-entry into the world of humans. This was not a how-to manual about living; it was a window into the unfolding of life, a mysterious alchemy as it slowly and intently reveals itself to us, both for our pleasure and our edification.

Spring // Cornelius

As we join our new form, it is like squeezing a boundless, open horizon into a small organic container. Each entry into the dense, pulsating resonance of the physical body is initially softened by gestation in the warm, fluid atmosphere of the female womb. The soothing, aqueous rhythms of this transitional environment help to ease the coming shock as intense, constrictive forces of this new medium take hold of our being. From this moment on, there exists a dynamic tension between our Essence and the interacting biological, psychological, and social dimensions that characterize this new milieu. These interactions take on very different qualities during each advancing season of life. As we evolve, the resonance of these ever-changing inner and outer circumstances becomes reflected in each unique field of consciousness, states of awareness that come to mirror the way we think, feel, and respond to life. Biological birth is the first of many passages yet to unfold during the lifespan. It is a seminal organizing event that establishes a template for the labor pains, stresses, and struggles that we face as we approach each new developmental threshold. The death-birth process is intrinsic to *all major* transformative crossings, and as we traverse the seasons, we are inevitably brought back to the earliest moments when we were pushed and pulled into a new dimension of being.

The equilibrium established between the Essential Self and that of the developing human identity maintains a critical balance that is necessary for any biological organism to function. During the course of our lifespan, we must first develop our capacities to effectively modulate the life force as it flows through our physical organism. Once these abilities are established, we will have many opportunities to enhance awareness of the ways in which these inner dynamics have become organized and influence all aspects of being. These vital forces have been given a variety of names, such as Light, Numina, Libido, Self, Life-Force, Holy Ghost, Essential Energy, Prana, Kundalini, or Qi. *We clothe these energies with images (God; Self) to make them accessible to consciousness, and the form these symbols take depends on the evolution of our relationship with them.* Some will spend many lifetimes deepening relationship to these inner processes, devoting entire pilgrimages to cultivating differentiated awareness of the many dimensions of being and energy, while others will live with little curiosity about the purpose of their lives or that which lies beneath the surface of their constructed identities.

Initially, we commit the greater part of our attention to the development of our physical capacities, our hearts, and our intellect. This is necessary for the growth of cognitive-emotional structures that enable this new house of the self to become stable and able to mediate between our internal and external experiences. Just as the transcendent Source-of-All-Being intentionally contracts to create space for the finite, immanent, material universe,[3] the larger Self provides the fertile ground from which a new, temporary center of identity and consciousness (ego) may be born from the depths of primordial oneness (see image below). *Our individual developmental process is but a microcosm of the larger story of creation. Born in the crucible of the primordial, maternal womb of undifferentiated unity, we hold within us the blueprint of all latent potentialities, as well as the impetus for the incarnating soul to awaken an array of universal qualities that we come to the human experience to mature.*

---

[3] Rotenberg, M. (2015). *The Psychology of TzimTzum, Self, Other, and God.* Maggid Books.

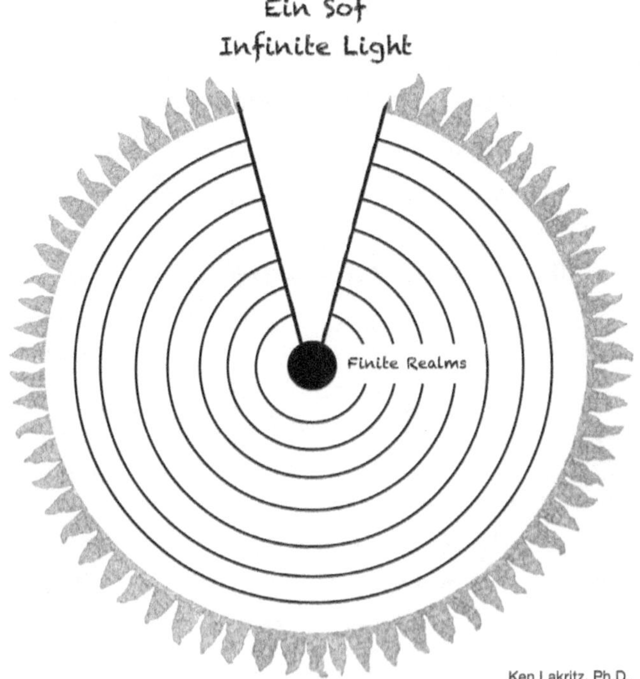

Within the *psychological pregnancy*[4] that follows the initial, *healthy* fusion between the human mother and infant, the ego, as an emerging complex,[5] arises dynamically from undifferentiated wholeness, like an island surfacing from the sea of the unconscious (see image below). To separate itself from the powerful gravity of the primordial maternal ground, this embryonic formation of the provisional[6] self must struggle heroically during the first seasons of life to establish its sovereignty as an

---

[4] Shany, L., Neumann, E. (2025). *The Theory*. Chiron Publications.

[5] "By ego I understand a complex of ideas which constitutes the centre of my field of consciousness and appears to possess a high degree of continuity and identity." Jung, C.G. [1921] 1971. *Psychological Types*. In *Collected Works of C.G. Jung*, vol. 6. Princeton University Press.

[6] Hollis, J. (1993). *The Middle Passage: From Misery to Meaning in Midlife*. Inner City Books.

autonomous psychic system and pole of conscious activity. *Over the course of the lifespan, we will become witness to many permutations in which the feminine principle of creation, birthing, interconnection, and receptivity and the masculine principle of differentiation, outer action, and the hero's journey are revealed through the arduous process of individuation.*[7]

Ego-Self Differentiation — Developmental Stages

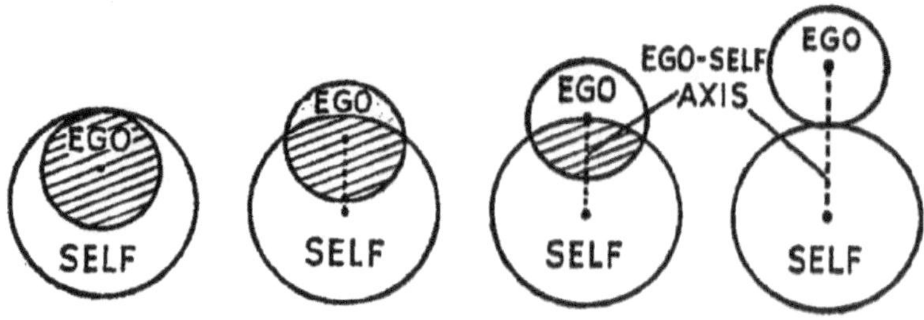

Edward Edinger
Ego and Archetype,
New York : Putnam, 1972.

As the Ego complex crystalizes during the initial stages of life, it becomes our first platform of awareness and functions as an interface for our interaction and immersion in the physical dimension. While some might say that the ego is an illusion to be transcended, overcome, or dissolved, it is, for practical purposes, an intrapsychic network crucial in the organized operations of the psyche as a whole. The healthy, dialectic relationship that evolves between the ego and Essential Self creates a *functional* (versus actual) duality that makes possible the differentiation and expansion of consciousness. The stable organization and fluid communication between these dual centers of consciousness (and identity) is also necessary for the mediation and balancing of the life force; the effective modulation of this

---

[7] Jung, C.G., Adler, G., Hull, R.F.C. (1996). *Collected Works of C.G. Jung,* Volume 7: "Two Essays in Analytical Psychology". Princeton University Press.

energy is requisite for us to adequately navigate the terrain of physical, psychological, and social life.

The ego, as an evolving *extension* of the Self, has a broad array of integral functions. Not only does this "organ"[8] of consciousness participate critically in the regulation of life force energies so that we can focus our thoughts and intentions, but it also makes possible the differentiation and integration of what is continually emerging from the depths. *It is the symbolic capacities of the psyche that make it possible to bring form to formlessness, to illuminate the numinous dimension of energy (Self) with image and archetype so that it can, then, be broken down into "digestible bites" (by the ego) and transformed into awareness. This "metabolic" process is the alchemy by which the Self becomes known to itself, the expansion of consciousness that we come into human existence to evolve.*

The nature and purpose of these psychic structures have always been subject to much debate. A developing ego that is over-identified with the powerful, primordial energy of the Source of Being will be challenged in its capacity to break free of its gravitational pull; this will hamper the ego's ability to presence and sustain conscious relationship with the Self as it increasingly makes its presence known to us later in life. The fully formed and cohesive ego is, furthermore, not meant to be a static identity or vessel; it is meant to be pliable enough to reorganize as the requirements of consciousness increase. Gradual transformation and strengthening throughout life allow the ego to transition from its role as primary identity to a conduit and channel for larger, transcendent awareness. When these polarities of the psyche (i.e., the ego and Self) are not in balanced relationship, however, they leave us, at one extreme, fragmented and flooded by the powerful gravitational pull of the Ground of Being, or, at

---

[8] Neumann, E. (1949). *The Origins and History of Consciousness*, originally published in German as *Ursprungsgeschichte des Bewusstseins* by Rascher Verlag, Zürich.

the other, squeezed off and suffocated from our vital energies by a rigid, resistant, and alienated predominating ego. Ultimately, we will not develop an effective and balanced relationship with these forces without the ego, first, becoming fully differentiated from the Self and well established and practiced within the evolving context of human life. *We must remember, however, that the ego complex is an extension – born from the womb of larger Self – and while it comes to experience itself as an autonomous, sovereign center of consciousness, it is and always will be subordinate to the Source of its creation.*

We must eventually come to understand the ways in which the tensions of interacting "physical" and "non-physical" states impact our newly developing organism. The form that the preliminary self takes is a direct reflection of the dynamic relationship that exists between the Essence and the physical body, embedded within the context of our chosen life circumstances. *Before we enter the human experience, we are fully in agreement with the choices that shape this coming life.* After we are born, however, a broader understanding of the conditions we have chosen for our evolution are no longer available to awareness. The meaning of that which lies behind the surface manifestation of human life is forgotten until we re-member and re-discover our deeper origins.

The springtime of human life requires a relatively long latency period, during which felt awareness of the original Source of Being remains mostly unconscious as the preliminary ego-self arises and struggles to differentiate from it. While connection with the core of who we are is never lost, the demands of this period of life require that the person fully unites with their developing organism and with those who will teach and care for them. As we grow in our new lives, palpable experience of the primordial energies from which we emerge becomes extremely subtle relative to the overarching demands and immersive pull of human physical, emotional, and intellectual development. It is like going into slumber, sensing that built into the fabric of our existence are innate, yet unconscious, instructions for gradual awakening.

When we choose those who give birth to us, the parents who raise us, and the family and culture that surround us, we create a foundation or platform for the trajectory of our lives. The interplay between our True Nature, biological predispositions, and the psychic makeup of those with whom we bond shapes the formation of character and the structure of the life that generates from it. In our original state, we know that we choose the ingredients of our lives with full awareness of the forms they take and the specific challenges they bring. During the course of life, however, it is very difficult to remain attuned to that which brings us meaning from a larger perspective. We do not specifically seek incarnations that are filled with bliss or good fortune, but rather, ones that are immersed in experiences that bring novel perspectives to our creative pursuits. *Bliss comes when we become aware that the course of life is in alignment with our original intentions.* Until the pieces of the puzzle of existence begin to coalesce during the latter periods of life, we must rely on *faith* as we ride intense and unpredictable rapids through the rugged terrains of our journey.

Total immersion in human life causes us, at first, to believe that we had no role in choosing the parents to whom we were entrusted, or the color of our skin or the form of our bodies. Many will say that they would not have chosen the life circumstances in which they now find themselves if they were really theirs to choose. Some will struggle to comprehend conditions that often feel to be at odds with their deepest desires and sensibilities. Questions might be asked such as: "Why would anyone choose parents who might harm them, or align with those persons and circumstances that create chaos and disharmony within our souls? What purpose does suffering and confusion serve in the formation of our choices and perspectives? How can anyone be responsible for a life that they believe was not theirs to choose or a life we feel we would not have chosen if we had the option?"

We may spend a good portion of our lives grappling with issues such as these, lost in the fog of daily survival, questioning the fundamental meaning of the way we invest our energies. Within the narrow lens of human awareness, it can be disheartening to lose touch with the grandness of the original intentions for our Soul's journey. As we walk the ground of the physical, all of humanity will struggle to comprehend the clear sense of purpose we carry for our lives before entering. As individual facets of a vast community of souls, we are like dusky crystals always seeking improved clarity so that we may ever more fully release the light that lies within. Each set of lived experiences adds further to our clarity and the evolving clarity of the whole. *The Soul's joy is not based upon the human principles of pleasure or pain, but on the infinite refinement and evolution of consciousness and the light that shines ever brighter within it.*

The platform built from the choices of our circumstances and the unlimited variety of perspectives experienced within human life provides a perfect medium for the refinement of that clarity. Gradual awakening of this core awareness is what gives us fortitude as we traverse the peaks and valleys of our pilgrimage through life. There are many road signs left by other pilgrims of past incarnations. They cannot inform us of the meaning of the choices that we have made for our unique journey; they can only give us clues as to how and when to recover the memories when the time is right to do so. Each of us must learn to accept that the pieces of a single life, though seemingly unconnected and without purpose, reveal themselves over time, not always in the form of direct awareness but, certainly, in the gradual refinement of our character.

The early period of our lives is like the hot housing of a sapling as each roots his or her heart in the secure and loving arms of the family while slowly, over time, spreading limbs and branches outward to the larger social world and culture. Although our original nature always remains intact and asserts itself as we define what is meaningful to us, our attention is initially drawn toward the establishment of secure bonds with others within this new world of biological form. From the moment of conception, we respond to the urgency of our vital needs with the appropriate measure of attachment to those on whom we are dependent for our survival. The merging of our personal field of consciousness with that of others is initially necessary for our adaptation and for the development of a preliminary human identity. The resulting patterns of thinking, feeling, and behavior form the basis for the regulation of life energy that flows through our organism. This conditioned self organizes the fundamental dynamics of our relationship to Essence and orchestrates the ways in which our subtle energies resonate within the physical body and become projected outwardly to the surrounding world.

While holistic and multidimensional in its properties, the physical shapes the formation and expression of biological organisms in predictable ways. Just as there are universal laws governing the nature of all matter, there are universal principles that affect the organization of thoughts, feelings, and behavior. The dynamic patterns that are generated from the way in which unique life circumstances interact within an organism play a central role in establishing the blueprint for the construction of the conditioned self. For the first half of life, learned forms of thinking, feeling, and behaving create attractions to certain modes of experience and perspective, modes that will, in turn, reinforce our expectations and views about the ways in which the world operates. The circular loop of these learned attractions and the self-fulfilling reinforcement of the experiences and perspectives that follow create a bubble of reality that repeats itself over and over throughout early life. This bubble is necessary for any adaptation and a feeling of predictability and control within our new environments. It will not begin to dissipate until the slowly intensifying experience of the Essential Self becomes more prominent in later life.

Because awareness of the Self remains dormant during this period, the experience of its energy remains very subtle relative to the dense experience of matter. The seemingly invisible nature of the numinous dimension leaves us with the question of its very reality and relevance. As we develop in our early lives, these questions may feel mostly philosophical and outside of our immediate interest and experience. This is so because our tasks within this period are largely to bond with primary others and develop our capacities to survive, adapt to, and navigate the outer terrain. These skills are a prerequisite for all initial and higher creative activities while in the human form. We cannot begin to relinquish our attention from the construction and crafting of the house of the preliminary self until we know that it can weather the demands and challenges of the tasks of adulthood.

Within the limited scope of human consciousness, we may not remember or recognize that the sensory splendors of the colors, sounds, shapes, textures, tastes, and qualities that comprise the landscape of the physical are gifts and legacies left by those souls who preceded us. The universe is replete with infinite vibrational possibilities. We are witness to this in the mountains, trees, animals, the sky, and the planets and stars around us. The organization of these elements that create the palpable experience of matter began first in thought form. The physical body was designed to sense, make meaningful sense of, and thoughtfully interact within this world of form. It is equipped with an armamentarium of sensors that allows us to process a full range of light and sound waves, to discern density and texture, and to appreciate the qualities of aroma and taste. Eyes, ears, and touch — all the senses — are necessary to translate and organize physical levels of vibrational information and for us to move about effectively and independently within this rich sensory medium.

The ebb and flow of life energy through the organism creates an awareness of a symphony of feelings and sensations that arise within specific centers or locations of the body. As with the constriction and dilation of the flow of blood through veins, this energy is similarly allowed or restricted by thoughts or states of awareness. Differing states of consciousness create a resonance through our beings like the strings of a musical instrument. When we bond with our parent(s), we initially unite with the resonance of those who love and care for us. This deep, dependent level of fusion allows another's state(s) of consciousness to begin to organize the flow of life energy through our being. Because of our necessary dependence upon others to, at first, orchestrate the flow of consciousness, the modulation of our thoughts and feelings is, initially, not our own and mirrors the ever-changing conditions, thoughts, and feelings of those around us. At this time, the stability of our experiences of ego-self is vastly influenced by external circumstances, and our early experience of Essential Self is that it is parental in nature and originates from outside of our conscious regulation.

The resonance that creates and is created by the dilation and constriction of life energy in the body-mind becomes mirrored in our emotional experiences and expressions. Emotions are a feedback system for the resonance created by our thoughts and the quality of consciousness that generates them. They also inform us about the ways in which thoughts administer the flow of energy within our organism. Emotions alert us about the safety and security of our environment, and they instruct us about the nuances of relationships with ourselves and others. Emotional awareness is the most important tool for appreciating the direction and impact of our own and other's intentions, as well as for discerning the text of the mystery of life as it unfolds. We must learn to read the signals of our emotional experience clearly, so that we may be able to navigate effectively through the dense vibrational forest that makes up the infinitely large and diverse landscape of human intentionality.

While a necessary aspect of development as we learn to master mental and physical capacities, our journey through the seasons involves the gradual realization that it is *we* who ultimately regulate the life energies that flow through us. The body-mind, however, is like a musical instrument that requires us first to learn the notes, chords, and variations. We must also determine when to go solo and when to play as a combo. The human tradition of apprenticeship evolved from an understanding that the youthful time of life should be a time of learning and mastery of all three physical, emotional, and intellectual capacities. When developing the instrument of the preliminary self, we must first learn to play the music of those composers who came before. As the experience of Essence becomes emergent in our awareness, we can then begin to become the creators of the music, of the forms that will be emulated by those pilgrims who will follow us. Until such time, those to whom our Souls are entrusted will write the melodies and the lyrics that play through us and shape our character. As we develop into the later seasons of life, it is eventually entirely up to us to cultivate new, larger dimensions of Self able to compose the songs, the stories that reflect what is most authentic and true to our being.

Our ability to guide the flow of Essential energy is first reflected in the higher capacity to direct the focus of our attention. As our brain develops, we also grow the capacity to call upon abstract images and symbols to form thoughts and plans. The evolving facility to utilize intention to guide the focus of thinking represents the first steps toward the independent and deliberate regulation of life force energy. Ultimately, our ability to consciously constrict (narrow) and dilate (expand) our focus enables us to tune into a variety of levels of awareness of ourselves and the world around us. This growing understanding of how to voluntarily shift in and out of a variety of states of consciousness allows our intentionality to work within subtler and subtler realms of creative expression.

To use a computer analogy, human beings operate within a continuous, simultaneous relationship between their hardware, software, and cloud. The "hardware" reflects the adaptive but hardwired operations and exigencies of physical being, including genetic predispositions and the essential drives to survive and procreate. The "software" is the plastic and programmable operating system that governs the cognitive-emotional-behavioral patterns that are shaped by life experiences within the context of the influence of the body's physiological processes. The software that is written by these experiences and processes eventually organizes a "provisional"[9] identity, a biographical self (which is local) that reflects our personal history within the sociocultural context of the world in which we find ourselves. The Cloud, on the other hand, derives from awareness that is numinal, transcendent of space-time, non-local, and rooted in transpersonal consciousness that exists before and after the hardware and software take form and exert their influence on our human lives. The *physical brain/body does not contain the Self*; however, it is the *local interface* by which *non-local* Being (soul/spirit) may interact within the matrix of material creation.

Our relationship to these three components of human functioning is in a continual process of flux and evolution. In the beginning of development, our intentions flow primarily from the hardware that is meant to support and ensure our survival. As our cognitive awareness and focus matures,

---

[9] Hollis, J. (1993). *The Middle Passage: From Misery to Meaning in Midlife.* Inner City Books.

our software comes online to formulate intentions that can begin to create beyond the pure and simple needs of ensuring the adaptation and perpetuation of the human species. Our creative abilities, however, continue to be governed by immediate social and cultural parameters until the Cloud or larger Self begins to enter conscious relationship with the other dimensions of being.

While numinous archetypal energies (i.e., a priori qualities, categories, images, and instincts) emanating from the Cloud shape and organize all levels of psychic functioning and experience, including the formation of the hardware and software,[10] *it is not until we establish a conscious relationship with the Source of these primordial blueprints that we can begin to evolve beyond their most basic forms, potentially maturing these primary, divine attributes (love, aggression, judgement, beauty, etc.) into increasingly wise expressions.* As we develop into later adulthood, we will continue to discover the roots of consciousness that live beyond the comprehension of the small self. Growing relationship with this greater field of perception holds the potential of informing all levels of being as a broader perspective of life comes into view. *Expanding awareness naturally transforms and updates old programming, making newly evolving operating systems possible. As we mature, software and hardware updates are necessary to adequately process the "quantum" level information emerging from the "Cloud" of deeper consciousness.* This consolidating experience of Self ultimately provides a new foundation for our intentions, particularly as our creations begin to evolve from an authentic center.

As children, we revel in these growing capabilities, playfully challenging ourselves to push the edges of our abilities to impact the world around us. The simple joy and awe of ourselves and of all creation fills our hearts with

---

[10] Mills, J. (2013). "Jung's Metaphysics". In *International Journal of Jungian Studies*, Vol. 5, No. 1: 19, 43.

inspiration as we become residents or citizens of the material dimension. Our task, as we grow, is to immerse ourselves fully in the lives that we have chosen, in whatever form or place that we have chosen them. As our bodies and minds operate more independently, we may eventually be able to consciously regulate and focus our life energies in ways that reflect what each of us uniquely intends for our evolution.

To create, we must first develop and organize the biological and psychological substrates of intentionality. Sensory translation of vibrational information, awareness of emotional resonance and how it mirrors the flow of subtle energy, and the ability to call upon the symbols of language to regulate the focus of attention are the biological foundations of our creative capacities. Throughout childhood and adolescence, our creative expressions are a manifestation of the dynamic relationship between developing physical and psychological capacities and how they organize and direct the flow of life energies.

During the springtime of life, the parameters of our intentions are mostly confined to the limits of biological, psychological, social, and culturally generated forms. Therefore, our initial creations are a reflection of early conditioning and the biological hardwiring that has evolved to maximize our chances of survival. This is so because the developing ego-self is preparing the necessary ground for the Essential Self to play a larger role later in our lives. The development of consciousness in this phase is substantially impacted by those key individuals who play a primary role in shaping our thoughts and character. Before we can create from a platform of greater awareness, we must first undergo a number of transformational experiences that require a gradual differentiation from those caregivers with whom we initially merge. Until that time, our thoughts, emotions, and the forms that we generate are an unconscious reflection of an identity organized and conditioned by the physical, social, and cultural environments in which we are immersed. While at first necessary and helpful to our survival and development, excessive attachment to these early constructions of self will leave us unprepared for the growing requirements of our evolution.

The wings of the butterfly can sustain flight only after they are strengthened by its struggle to free itself from the cocoon. This is also so for the human organism as it develops from infancy to adulthood. From the very beginning, we are always challenging our capacities for solo flight. Built into our organismic programming are our original instructions, which gradually call upon us to strive to transcend the limitations of our human conditioning and evolutionary, biological drives. This effort ultimately arises from an inner impetus to achieve expanding awareness that enables us to operate from a larger ground of Being. This is accomplished in stages, however, only as each layer of biological, psychological, and spiritual development unfolds.

The foundation of emotional security makes it possible to gradually leave the nest of youth and opens us to the greater freedoms and responsibilities of adulthood. The process of leaving this early life structure can manifest in a multitude of forms and depends upon the nature of bonds with those who have loved and cared for us. Very powerful internal and external forces often entice us to return to the security of childhood while simultaneously calling us to move forward to fulfill our not-yet conscious destinies. Woven within the growing fabric of life are the threads of past attachments and experiences. They are the backdrop from which we orient ourselves toward the dawning light of the future. Throughout our lives, experiences continually remind us that, as we reach to the sky for our hopes and dreams, we are always standing upon the shoulders of every soul who has ever come before.

The subtle call from the life force only gradually introduces us to our essential qualities as they begin to enter more fully into the matrix of our life and relationships. While wondrous and meaningful, emergent energy emanating from our authentic core can become a significant source of stress as it progressively builds and reveals itself throughout the lifespan. Steadily breaching consciousness as we mature into adulthood, this growing presence can shake the very foundations of the preliminary identity and the life that has developed from it. Initial encounters with expanding awareness can be disorganizing and call into question the very basis of an already created reality. As it slowly gathers, however, it offers the gradual gift of realization that there are many levels and perspectives from which existence may be viewed and experienced.

Stresses inherent in the unfolding of consciousness are often viewed from a framework of health or illness. Many older traditions better understand that life transitions supported by initiations are necessary for crossing thresholds of consciousness, particularly as we leave behind old life structures and open to new territories of awareness and development. They realize that, without proper efforts to midwife the soul's birth through new stages of life, unnecessary suffering can become pervasive as fear and resistance naturally arise when attempting to cope with normal processes of transition and reorganization. Fearful of losing footing within our shifting identities, most of us understandably attempt to attenuate the powerful echoes of emerging consciousness; we learn many ways to resist or defend against the call of expanding awareness as it continues to open us to the vulnerability of our authentic core. When experienced, and initiated pilgrims or helpers are not present, there is no cultural mechanism to facilitate the awakening Soul into enlarging consciousness. Consequently, some will have to find their way alone through the dark, stormy corridors of these transitions without support or guidance. This will ask something more of them and require enormous courage and faith while navigating unaided through the wilderness periods of life without a map or a compass.

The courage to listen to the subtle voice that lies within gives a heroic quality to the process of discovering our true origins. The first developmental shifts are but a taste of what's to follow in the fall and winter phases. We begin by walking, then dressing and feeding ourselves. Slowly, we rely more and more on our own judgment and choices. Our developing capacities make it possible to begin to stand on our own without the continued presence, support, and input of older pilgrims.

The inner voice we begin to carry into life, while not yet fully our own, is increasingly able to begin its creative expression and adapt to the emerging tasks and demands of adulthood. This voice is the siren's call that beckons each individual to follow the road that no one else can or must take but us.

Spring // Shemah

Looking back, I have begun to view my life almost entirely as a story about Love. It is a story of love for my parents, my brothers, friends, wife, companions, children, grandchildren, and the unexplainable love that called me to risk expanding beyond fear into new and ever-evolving awareness. It is also a story about discernment and learning to listen to the inner guiding voice that illuminates the path ahead. This is not to say that my life was devoid of great suffering. My suffering was, at times, intense, deep, and without relief. Yet, it was suffering that opened my eyes to something larger than myself and brought me closer to an awareness of the shared plight of humanity, of which I eventually discovered I was a part. I began to view human suffering, my suffering, not as an absence of love but as an integral part of the love that has called and opened me to deeper realms of my Self.

I will try to remember through the eyes of a child and a young man as I recount the moments of my life. Yet, I find it difficult to refrain from infusing my memories with the perspective of an old man, who increasingly held his life with such a profound sense of wonder and gratitude. As I advanced in age, I also grew in the realization of the tenderness of life and of the challenge of maintaining equilibrium, joy, inner spaciousness, and perspective in the face of life's complexities and stresses. It is always easy to evaluate our lives in hindsight and to forget what it was like to walk through the dense emotional landscape — to choose, to express, to love, and to just be present to the joys and vast sufferings of self and others — without a map or a guide or a memory of our original intentions before arriving in this earthly reality. I come to this place with few answers. But I have arrived with an abundance of awe for the miraculous process of unfolding, of expanding, of co-creation, of the synchronicities that give clues about the inner workings of things, and the eternal spark that hungers for awareness, for experience, and for understanding. This spark that burns within has given me the courage to use whatever tools that were at my disposal to plunge further and further into the mystery of living.

My gestational beginnings were not unlike those of many others. I was the product of a healthy pregnancy. But like some others of my time, I was exposed to a life-threatening bacterium upon my arrival that left me separated from my mother, and a necessary level of human touch, for almost two weeks. I have often pondered the reasons for this and the effect it had upon my emotional constitution and feeling of security. This early physical isolation also left me feeling separated from life, sometimes so disconnected that I felt like an alien among humans. As I grew toward adulthood, I wasn't sure to which world I belonged, or to which one I wished to belong. I have always, on some level, lived in both worlds, straddling two distinct realities that I have worked a lifetime attempting to bring together. I have struggled my whole life wishing to enter and, paradoxically, discovering that the further I inhabited my life, my identity, and my body, the closer I felt to that tender being that sustained me during the weeks of quarantine. I learned very early that when the so called "outer world" was not available to sustain me, there was an immutable inner reality, an interior-core, which was not subject to the same conditions of my outer life. So began my path, my struggle, to hold the tension between the sustaining love of my "inner" reality and the human love that nurtured me so that I could engage whatever destiny was mine to fulfill.

There is no question that my early life was built upon a foundation of love. Even with the trauma of segregation from my mother at birth, I was eventually wooed into the arms of my parents by their tenderness and love. The effects of those early moments of separation were more immediately overcome by my innate, instinctual inclination to move toward that which provided a felt sense of safety, security, sustenance, and a close approximation of my origins in love. I have been wooed by love my entire life to enter and to go further into the mysteries of being human. Yet, the character and nature of that which drew me, and that which continues to entice me to risk moving beyond the familiar and secure, underwent a very fascinating evolution as my life unfolded. The miracle of life, I found, was revealed in the gradual uncoiling of the Self, a process involving the continuous disassembling and re-assembling of life structures that provided the progressive foundations upon which my consciousness was able to expand and coalesce.

Remembering my life, I find myself flashing back and forth between the perspective of a child and that of an experienced adult, parent, and grandparent into which I eventually matured. I am giving myself this license, because all the moments of my life continue to live within me and can be accessed from various points of view. Much of my experience was characterized by times of needed surrender and times of intentful action, a process of learning to discern when to be receptive and when to act decisively. We are born with such an intrinsic sense of our freedom of will and of that which is our truest nature. For that reason, my entire being initially resisted the overwhelming biological forces that so powerfully took grip of this nature as I grew. These forces eventually thrusted me into a lifelong symbiotic relationship with the physical and emotional bodies that enabled me to enter and adapt to my new reality. Early experiences of my internal core were now being overshadowed by the much less subtle experience of my bodily needs and intellectual development. The complex nature of this new sensory environment required the ability to process and organize incoming waves of information and to attune myself to the intricate web of emotional signs and signals. The consuming demands of my new human life certainly dominated my experience for some time and, lamentably, left me without a memory or feeling of connection to my original nature.

At that time, I felt overwhelmingly drawn toward that which provided comfort and soothing of both my emotional and bodily distress. I also became captive to the powerful, instinctual drives that so quickly and automatically responded to my immediate existential circumstances. Initially "trusting" that I was in loving hands, there was little choice but to surrender to and abide by these early conditions. Our brains and bodies are amazingly designed to know just how to lay the groundwork for early development, and we hope that we are met on the other side by parents of intelligence, wisdom, and love. As a parent myself, I remember that helping my children become successful members of the family and community remained in the forefront of my initial priorities. My commitment to these fundamentals was, I hope, balanced by my striving to also remain aware of the Souls that were now in my hands to care for the best way l could.

It took me many years to begin to understand my struggle as I moved through and emerged from childhood. What was once pure Essence was now joined with a biological form with its own unique ancestry, appearance, and biological proclivities. As I bonded with those who were to become my parents, I seamlessly adopted and internalized their needs, inclinations, and perceptions of who I was and how to be a member of this new world. I have continually asked myself if this primal attachment is born purely of instinct or if the essence of a parent's love is inherently an invitation to the new soul to enter the miracle and mystery of life's journey? The parental bond — that can so closely approximate the love that we knew before entering the body — is a gift, I believe, that can only truly be returned as we look into the eyes of our own children. Without this divine flow of loving energy from one being to another, I know that I would not have been receptive to others to shape my character to conform to the expectations of my new human circumstances. I have often seen children who were mistreated and forgotten, who withdrew from outer life and armored themselves from connection with it. They taught me that, without love, care, and safety, it is extremely difficult to bring our inner lives forward into the world of others. *When the invitation of love is not present, I find it hard to fathom why we would take the risk to open the "temple gates" of the inner sanctum of Being. The "open doorway" to the soul is clearly a prerequisite for building the foundations necessary for the S/self to evolve, and, without this opening, we remain cloistered in a world of forces that sustain us but preclude our full potential for flowering.*

So, like a duckling that follows those who imprint upon it the first biological, psychological, social connection, I followed my parents into life.

So many elements of my first experiences of love did seem to transcend the conditionalities that are such a reality of human existence. In retrospect, however, I realize that I was also in training to become a member of the human world with its many conditions and contingencies. I was being groomed to function with sensitivity and attunement to the expectations of my household, culture, and social environment. I cared about what others thought and sought to be a part of and to please those important to me. Nonetheless, I always felt the tension of having to adapt my impulses to fit the priorities of the world around me. I also often wanted to place the cart before the horse when it came to my personal development. I frequently wished or imagined that I was already complete and no longer in need of guidance, resorting to fantasies in which there were no limitations to my powers, where I was not bound by the laws and rules of earthly life. Able to express my innermost impulses and feelings through play and fantasy, I found solace and a sense of equality there. My imagination allowed me to retain some semblance of freedom and a memory of something eternal, something almost forgotten, where there did not exist such a differential power between the adults and me.

Like many who are subject to the conditionalities of being human, I took the limitations and contingencies placed upon me very personally. As a young adult, I was often resentful of the ways in which my thoughts and feelings were shaped by early life and of the family vulnerabilities that I came to feel had been passed down through the generations for me to unwittingly shoulder. I could not see the trajectory that my life was taking and could not have begun to appreciate the great task that parents face while helping a new life develop a solid foundation. It would be many years before I could understand that, as parents, we are still so unfinished, so unexamined, and not particularly in control of our own lives either. I wanted to be free, to be whole, and to be independent. I also wanted to bypass the steps that I had to take to build upon the ground that would eventually allow me to reach the wholeness of which I dreamed. Fortunately, I did not take the bypass route. Somehow, I discovered that, when I took shortcuts or resisted the necessary developmental tasks before me, I ended up not closer but further away from myself. I think that it was this basic understanding that guided me and eventually enabled me to accept my own vulnerability and to appreciate that I was here to learn and that there was a lot of it to do.

Having given myself over to this life, to identify with this person named Shemah, I grew to become a physically healthy young man who had learned the rudiments of navigating my natural and social environments. By pre-adolescence and adolescence, the subtle center of Self that had laid dormant while I was developing physically and learning the basics of being human, slowly began to unfold in my experience like a moon just beginning to wax. With a nascent awareness of my individuality and ability to engage the world around me more independently and reasonably, I felt as if I were waking from a dream that sustained me while I was establishing the "sea legs" that would enable me to engage the expectations and responsibilities of becoming a member of the human community. I began to feel increasingly in charge of my life, not knowing until much later that my ability to consciously choose and direct my life energies was only in its infancy. The choices I would make clearly reflected a template that had been established during early periods of my development. Awareness of these patterns was not yet available for conscious self-determination, nor should it have been at this time of life. But as far as I was concerned, I was in charge of my life.

The basics of my conditioning, now complete, lived a life of their own. I was a self-regulating being that could operate increasingly in the world without the constant guidance of older people. This was an empowering revelation that I was no longer completely dependent upon others to direct my energies.

This was the first of many re-alignments of identity that would eventually transport me to a growing experience of what lay at my depths. I began to realize that this increasing sense of agency, rudimentary as it was, was providing me with footing that had never existed before — new levels of organization that would eventually allow for something to blossom within me that would, one day, help me to better understand the nature of who I am.

As with most teenagers and pre-adults, I had an unrealistic and inflated sense of my own independence and awareness. Thinking back to what was to confront me as I entered the adult world, I can't imagine how we could engage the overwhelming task of these major transitions if we knew exactly how deep, and occasionally dark, the waters ahead can be. I often miscalculated that my emotional maturity matched my intellectual development and believed that I was more ready to stand on my own than I actually was. My fundamental capacities were fully developed, but my maturity — my judgment, my sense of responsibility, my empathy and compassion — was much slower to evolve. I was socially awkward and anxious and wasn't at all sure how to extend my trust, my heart, to my peers in the hope of making meaningful connections. I was beginning to expand my emotional attachments to those outside of my immediate family in a gradual effort to see if I could sustain myself beyond the nest that had so long supported me. I was testing the skills incubated in early life to see if my wings were strong enough to carry me on my own.

Survival during this period of my life required that the majority of my attention be devoted outwardly to ensure that I was able to acclimate to my new environment. While carrying me through the tender days of my entry into human life, the earlier, palpable experience of Essence was now almost silent and had become relegated to the imaginal realms of childhood. Those early experiences of Self, now confined to the ephemeral, the ineffable, the intuitive, would become as essential for me to thrive later in life as my attention to physical and social development had been in my youth. My rational capacities were growing, and what was becoming "real" to me, and to those with whom I now shared my "reality," were those elements of life that could be felt, seen, heard, tasted, and subjected to consensual and social validation.

As I entered my adolescence, my feeling of autonomy provided the illusion that I was beginning to stand on my own. I did not realize, nor would I have admitted, that the platform on which I stood and from which I was beginning to launch, was not fully of my making. The "family ground," as I call it, provided me with the support and guidance from which I could test my capacities for creating a new base of my own — one that would someday be able to support a life independent from my parents. Struggling deeply with an inner ambivalence, however, I was fearful of opening my heart to a new kind of love, a love that did not hold within it the same kind of security as my early attachments had offered. I felt a pull to move forward but would often find myself reaching back for the comfort of my early life or searching outward in vain for the kind of primal bonds I felt as a child. I had yet to realize that I was entering a vastly different arena of relationships, one that was not meant to ease my landing into this new level of life as the qualities of my first ones had.

I believe my parents provided me with everything I truly needed to begin the first big separation from my family of origin. Not all were as prepared, and unprepared, for leaving the nest as I was. Even though we are all met with the task of differentiating ourselves from the foundations of our youth, some, I found, have felt a need to tear free, to assert themselves in more extreme and creative ways to establish a sense of self they could call their own. We were all looking for something to set us apart from others and, most particularly, our parents. This striving to begin to have a selfhood of my own, to manifest something deeper within, appeared also to be brought forward by an innate awareness of the need to establish an identity that was uniquely mine. This slowly evolving and ever-transforming experience of my inner terrain would eventually make possible a conscious awareness of the something forgotten that was gradually re-emerging in my experience.

As far as I can remember, a tension always existed between what lay at my core and the family constellation with which I joined not long after birth. For the greater part of my childhood and early adulthood, I struggled deeply with the felt contrasts between these vastly different poles of awareness. Not until later in my adulthood was I able to comprehend how this tension was integral to my unfolding. While I honored what my parents provided for me, I was unsettled and angry, feeling pressure to align with values and beliefs that were not consistent with what was arising within me. I felt called to engage in the very scary and sometimes dangerous task of leaving the familiar territory of youth to set sail for the unknown shore of an adulthood that seemed to be moving upon me quickly.

I found myself devaluing my parents and began disenfranchising myself from the very support that had carried me into early adulthood. Throughout much of my early life, I believed that we really could leave or tear free from the conditions and conditioning of youth. I was intent on defining myself as distinct from my family and attempted to leave behind that which I later came to realize, for good or for bad, was irreversibly etched in the recesses of my thoughts, feelings, and character. I was anguished that I felt forced to contend with the unfinished, or should I say the unconscious, family struggles that by default were now mine to carry. I felt unfairly burdened and no longer willing to carry such a weight that I begrudgingly believed was not mine to hold. As we "break free" of our family of origin, however, we naively believe that we have moved beyond the gravitational pull of our early conditioning. *I can see now that we continue to return to the "scene of the crime" of our childhood only to repeat old patterns over and over again to process the past until we have sufficient consciousness to actually move on from it.*

I gradually came to realize that, as humans, we are never finished. We often bring new beings into our lives before we ever reach true maturity and, certainly, before we come to understand our roles as parents. I carry deep regrets for some of the ways in which I impacted and shaped my own children. Yet, I know that, for the most part, I gave them what I was able to give and did my best to provide the basics of what they needed to thrive and eventually become their own people. The wonderful and arduous job of preparing my children for the great challenges of life often overshadowed my ability to be a good witness to what was emerging in them. I frequently lost sight beyond the immediate life skills I was working so hard to help them build and, therefore, was not always able to be the best observer of their deeper movements and feelings.

Ironically, my fundamental task as a parent became the project of bestowing upon them the very conditioning with which I grappled as a child, and with which my own children would also struggle on their way to discovering who they were. It was my job, I felt, to help prepare them for a very complex and difficult world in which the gravity of life would eventually become their new teacher.

I often felt great sadness that this priority was often at odds with being in-tune with what was most important to them at certain periods of their lives. My priorities as a parent and my priorities as a child were rarely in concert with one another. As a parent, I felt that it was my job to provide the ground on which my children could solidly stand and from which they would have to push to tear free. As an adolescent, it was my job to take the very difficult steps to emancipate from my family and begin to discover who I was within a world of billions of souls who were also searching for who they were as well.

The process of growing toward early adulthood was by no means a linear one. It was often one step forward and two steps back, with frequent excursions off the main path to unexpected delights, dead ends, and dangerous roads. Until I became a parent, I could not have even imagined the responsibilities and pressures that my parents held so that my attention could be freed to learn the basics of becoming a human being. Beneath me, like the roots of a tree, I sensed that the core of who I am was always there to catch me when the shifting sands of my human identity became particularly tenuous. Yet, I also discovered that it was my human bonds that sustained me so that I could endure the challenges and anxieties of living in a complicated world in which my perception of myself and others seemed to always be in flux.

The subtle inner Essence of who I was remained just that, subtle, at this time of my life. It was the outer identity, the foundations of my physical, intellectual, emotional, and social skills and capacities, that was my primary base of operation and sense of who I was. From this, I was able to launch into life as a student, a friend, and eventually a lover. In the background of my consciousness, I sensed that there was more to this person named Shemah than what appeared on the surface. Over time, I have become clearer that there are so many layers to our lives that support us, structures and levels that must be established first before we are able to excavate the gold that lies at our center. My impatience to find this inner treasure often caused me to dig too deeply and too fast, searching to understand the roots and mysteries of my life before I had assembled the outer scaffolding necessary to sustain this deeper awareness. It also has been this desire to behold what exists beyond the surface layers that has enticed me to move forward through my fears to endure the necessary sufferings that naturally come as the veil of life is lifted.

Fortunately, I was graced to find other, wiser individuals who shined a guiding light for me as I walked through the darkest valleys of my journey. The hubris that helped me to have the courage to create the first "separate" sense of identity was no longer of much assistance as my adult journey unfolded. I found that I would have to relinquish this bravado for a more receptive mode of engaging the challenges in my life. Throughout my early and middle adulthood, I was enormously privileged to have the friendship and guidance of those who had successfully crossed the most challenging chasms of life.

"How does one navigate these crossings?" I often thought; "How do we move from one place to the next along a pathway requiring that we evolve in our depth, maturity, and awareness?" I am reminded of the power of "mirroring" in giving us our first stable images of ourselves. My parents were the first "human mirrors" that so effectively shaped how I began to see and experience myself. The physical, reflective, and social mirrors played a greater role in my later childhood and adolescence. During that period, I began to identify more strongly with my physical image and the often-overpowering emotional experiences that shaped my reactions to life. Yet, as I approached early adulthood, there came a time when the notion of mirroring took on a whole different quality for me. At that time, to be "mirrored" meant to be "seen," to be understood, and to be valued for something more true and subtle in myself. This eventually enabled me to begin to see myself more deeply and to value that which was stirring within my own inner life. This was the beginning of my appreciation that there were modes of experience beyond what was apparent to my usual capacity of perception. I would often ask myself, "Was there a larger meaning to our lives than we could comprehend?"

It was those first "seers," who could penetrate beyond the surface, who initiated me into new dimensions of my life. The many experiences that followed would eventually enable me to also be a witness for others. Without those who lovingly made themselves available to "witness" me, I would not have been able to move successfully across the many fateful and difficult transitions that would follow. It is this love and regard for and from my fellow travelers that has continued to encourage me further along my path. It is they who ultimately helped to foster the courage and awareness to create a life within which I could eventually discover, or should I say re-discover, the nature of who I am.

SUMMER

Shemah (1958)

My deeper intelligence gives little rein when it comes to my education in faith. As time stretched, those earlier moments, when inner hands held and lifted me from the abyss, faded again into the cedar woodworks of my awareness like the voice of a muted background singer. I continued to actively avoid the gravitational pull of my heart's essence from sheer embarrassment of my sensitivity, vulnerability, and native depth. My resistance to the inner laws of being, however, eventually succumbed to a schooling by Newton's outer laws of gravity.

It was 1958. I was 31, and my 51' Chevy 3100 cherry red truck was in dire need of repair. It was my pride and joy and the envy of my friends. In an old, dilapidated warehouse at the industrial edge of town, I began searching down the isles for a new camshaft while workers labored to restock the shelves. Smelling of oil fumes and old moldy cardboard, I traversed rows of discarded and forgotten gems that powered vehicles which would one day become *"classics." Without warning, a large box of heavy engine parts teetering at the shelf's edge suddenly fell from above, crushing my head in a blow. Blood pouring from my lacerated scalp, I fell to the floor nearly unconscious and in excruciating pain, only later to realize the seriousness of the injuries sustained to my neck and back. In that moment, the course of my life changed instantly and permanently. I asked myself, "Why me? Why now?" Had I believed in God, I might have conjured a reason for His wrath. Through the pounding of the pulses in my ears, I heard a familiar voice within, the voice of an old friend who never failed to come forward from the depths in times of suffering and confusion, say, "This is simply a course correction. You are not wise, willing, or able enough to make this change without the unseen hand."*

My "accident" left a severe injury to my C6-C7 cervical spine, with the great fortune of no lasting paralysis. A physically muscular young man, seemingly in control of my life, I attempted to return to business as usual only to discover that I could no longer do the usual. Pain and discomfort became my constant companions while I fought and attempted to work around these permanently altered life parameters. I could no longer sit for stretches of time working at my oak desk, nor lift the engine parts necessary to restore my beloved Chevy truck. My suffering ground down my tiring defenses like a milestone mashing wheat into flour until surrender was no longer an option but a state of being.

Unlike my earlier spiral, however, this tempest jettisoned me squarely on a deeply vulnerable, tender, and ineffable core that had been sealed over for years, but never absent, the impact striking so hard that the self-glued seal began to splinter. One dark, winter evening while reading Simone Weil's Waiting for God, the night lights shimmering in the valley below my hillside bungalow, a piercing brilliance filled my vision. "It is time for me to show you my true appearance," a familiar voice echoed through the fraying threads of my facade. A light-being came forward into my mind's eye: "You are strong enough now to see me as I am," Cornelius said to me. Confused but open, I sheepishly replied, "Ok, I think I am." Indescribable grace filled me as the light flowed from Cornelius within me, permanently illuminating the recesses that had been hidden from view. Given no more reason to fade, Cornelius became a conscious, steady, and chosen companion, preparing me for what was to come as I approached midlife.

I was 35 when "the calling" came. It arrived in the form of a dream:

> *In the shadow of a smoldering volcano, I sat in preparation with other students waiting for the master's call. I was summoned to a small cabin in a beautiful forest where the master lied on his death bed. He prompted me to come close so he could whisper in my ear. He asked that I succeed him as "master of the good name," as his life was coming imminently to a close. I remember feeling overwhelmingly honored, undeserving, and unprepared. I was told that I had 24 hours to provide my answer or the nearby volcano would erupt and destroy the valley and all of its inhabitants.*

I awoke from the dream in tears, knowing that I had been called to a responsibility of great weight and significance. I also was aware of the consequences of not accepting the master's request. My soul was calling me forward to realize a purpose for which the ego certainly had no purview. Past experiences taught me the cost of failing to stay true to my soul's intentions. Despite the bumpy challenges of returning to the center, the soul, through the deep, well-trodden, self-etched grooves I had worn into my path, I would not make this mistake again. To myself, I said, "Yes," surrendering to the master's request.

Summer // Author

As I listened to Shemah, the contrasting elements and the common, intertwining threads of his process through the transcendent and the immanent speak to the challenges of how we discover meaning within the thick of our lives. We often reach for defining answers about the super-ordinate nature of life, only to find that these answers come up short unless they are complimented by direct experiences within the felt process of living. An elder friend of mine recently wrote eloquently about the meaning and challenges as we confront the ending of our lives. Now more immediately faced with the reality that he is reaching the end of his own life, when reminded of a passage he had written, he remarked, "Did I really write that?"[11] The I that observes and seeks meaning and the I that lives-through, while one in the same, each contributes to life's perspective in unique and tangible ways. Without a map, we may get lost when we enter a new territory, but without entering and experiencing the territory, the map is only a piece of paper with lines and words.

Summer // Cornelius

When we are born, we open entirely to a symbiotic relationship with other more experienced and, if we have chosen, loving human beings. Our souls depend upon these attachments for our physical, emotional, and mental capacities to flourish. As we develop into adulthood, growing autonomy

---

[11] Huston Smith, personal communication

gradually enables us to release from total fusion with others. Initially, this merging of fields of consciousness makes possible the creation of secure bonds with the world of other human beings and the stable organization of our relationship to our Essence. The regulation of this energy is patterned from these initial alliances and forms the basis for all unconscious and conscious intentionality in the next phase of our lives. Yet, until we begin to awaken to the roots of who we are, we experience the control and creation of our reality as originating from outside of us.

Like milk from the breast, our first human bonds provide a palpable connection to the "food," to the "oxygen supply," of Essential energy. Early experiences cause us to perceive that the source of this "oxygen" originates from those with whom we form these initial attachments. Within the recesses of our organismic programing, we innately know that without this "feeding" and fusing of life energies with our early caregivers, we would fail to thrive within our new corporeal form. In the absence of loving, devoted, and consistent care, we either wither as if we were a plant without water or withdraw into protective shells that make connection with other human beings very challenging and painful. These conditions were created in order that we remain close to these loving others so that they may help us survive and adapt to the potentially dangerous physical and emotional conditions of early life. Primary human attachments establish the initial experience that the presence, or absence, of Life Force energies are, in part, dependent upon our emotional connections with others. This perception is a necessary aspect of balancing our growing autonomy with the realization of mutual dependency, an awareness of interdependency that is highly valued both for its role in our continued evolution and for the immense joy of shared connection.

Entering the summertime of life, we encounter strong impulses to begin to push free from the first platform of life. We feel like a fledgling ready to fly from the nest to challenge our newfound strengths and capacities. With each independent step, we discover new pieces of our emerging identity as a separate being. Awakening from the dependence of early relationships, we develop our own nascent abilities to open to and modulate life-force energies. It is a wonder and considerable challenge to fully honor the life from which we emerge and honor our growing awareness and alignment with the life that is ours alone to create. Each season of life asks us to take an increasing role in our participation with the flow of Being. We can resist or unite with the progressive movements that continually call attention to our inner life, but without evolving awareness of the responsible relationship we hold to these processes, we will be unable to direct the focus of our intentions consciously.

Transition into adulthood involves gradual release from the first platform. Courage and fortitude are required as we face the ambivalent, conflict-filled journey to leave the shore of our early life to search for a new place to call home. We quickly discover that we are not able to endure the troubled seas of existence without an adequate vessel to keep us from being pulled under by life's powerful undertows. We have yet to discover and integrate into awareness our continuous, independent, nuanced regulation of life energies. When first transitioning from our primary relationships, we often continue to perceive that the essence of love derives entirely from our intimate connection with others (see next image). While they may offer a portal or calling to this experience, it is not until the fall and winter periods of life that we are meant to discover that *others* are not responsible for opening and closing our heart to this energy. In the early summertime of life, our perception continues to be that our relationships hold the key that opens and closes access to the doorways of love that unconditionally resides within the matrix of Being. While this draws us close to others, this belief ultimately leads us to feel as if the experience of love is conditional and subject to the fleeting and impermanent circumstances of human relationships.

Perceived Source of Love

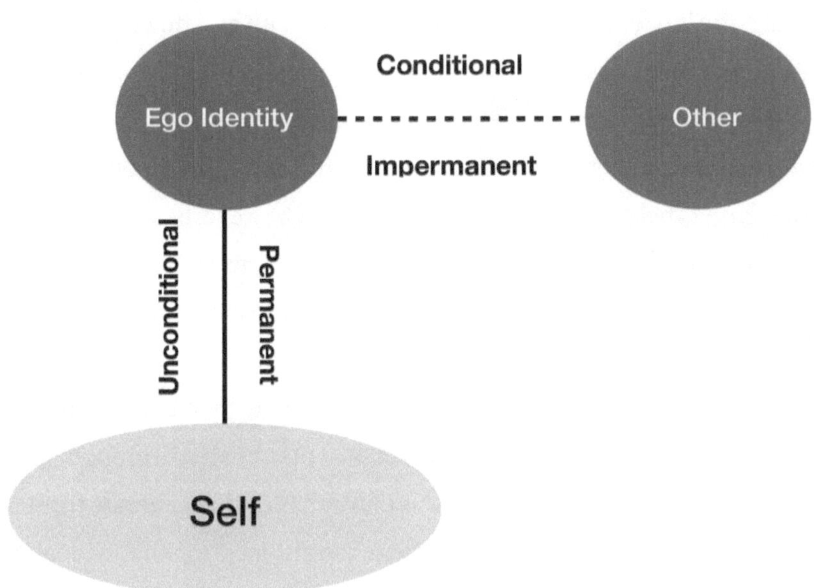

Ken Lakritz, Ph.D.

The perception that access to our inner depths is enabled only through connection with others continues to provide a powerful impetus for reestablishing new foundations of primary human relationships. Unaware that we are now traversing untraveled territories of the human heart, we carry with us our earlier agenda of complete, unconscious fusion with others as an attempt to reproduce our first model of human relationships. The search for Beloved Other(s) represents a major turning point in our development. It sets the stage for a collision between the unconditioned and the conditioned, heaven and earth, which begins to awaken us to the realization of mutuality as we discover that others are looking to us also as a doorway to the inner sanctum of Being.

As we build a bridge to the second platform, our yet-to-be conscious relationship to the movements of subtle energies will continue to reflect our early conditioning. A unique homeostasis has established itself in the various centers of our body by the time we reach adulthood. Like the notes of a flute, the life force dances back and forth and up and down through the multitude of openings or body centers in a harmony that is unique to the ways in which our being has become organized. Our resonance represents the distinctive manner in which it moves within and through our organism to the larger field of consciousness in which we are immersed. The resulting structure and form of the second platform reflects the patterns and harmonies of our distinct character that was shaped during the earlier, springtime of our lives.

Openness or resistance to others is mirrored by their openness or resistance to us; the worlds of interactions that coalesce around us are directly shaped by the specific patterns of resonance that generate from our being. We are not conscious yet of these conditioned inclinations, as this is a time for complete identification with our physical body and patterns of thinking, feelings, and behaviors. The second platform is built upon biographical "ingredients," which steer our lives in a direction destined to attract certain persons, opportunities, and experiences. As a reflection of the inner balance of our relationship to Self, the resonance we generate determines with whom we join, the work we choose, and virtually all manners of intentionality and creation that we pursue. During the course of our lives, we may discover that life platforms provide the perfect trajectory for the refinement of each unique perspective and character.

The first period of life involves bonding with humanity and feeling ourselves to be human; the second period is concentrated on entering the community and establishing a place within the human tribe; and the third, fall period, provides circumstances for a greater balance of conscious alignment with a growing awareness of Self. The pivotal task within the summer period of life is to begin to awaken to the dual nature of both our current identification with the conditioned self and our roots within a larger experience of our origins. This building experience of our depths enables a growing sensitivity to the needs of others and an emerging awareness of the multitude of perspectives that exist within our shared reality. As we expand, our eyes naturally open to the distinctness and separateness of others. What began as a preconscious experience of unity now grows into an awareness of diversity, of multiplicity, requiring a transition to a more active and intentful giving as well as receiving.

This is a time of actively searching for those with whom we wish to begin to build an adult life. Pursuit of the Beloved Other(s) is like a calling or a song that resonates outward in search of a matching harmony, a vibrational dance that synchronizes both of us along the various points at which the flow of Essential energy joins with our bodies. The chemistry that unites us with the Beloved is a doorway that opens us to transcendent oneness with the Source of Being and, simultaneously, to the immanence of our conditioned, unconscious patterns of thinking and feeling. The alchemical interplay of our connection to the Beloved also gives us greater access to the dance of the masculine and feminine energies, an outward tension of opposites that had been mostly dormant until the late springtime of life. Only within this dance of opposites, of the masculine and feminine, the unconditioned and the conditioned, will we have the mirror needed to awaken us to the specific nature of our unconscious ways of being. Until we become aware of the precise manner in which our thoughts, feelings, and behavior orchestrate the flow of life energies, we are not able to play a more active, intentful, and self-determining role in the creation of our reality.

Awakening from the egocentric haze of childhood, we now have opportunities to become more attuned to the needs of others and the realization that adult relationships require a balanced give and take of energies. An important human teacher once referred to the notion of the "middle way,"[12] which acknowledges that life within the human body requires a balanced attention to the dual sides of our nature. Our desire to join the Beloved stems partly from an ever-continuing wish to return to an unconscious state of unity. The blending of adult souls, however, quickly transitions from the transcendent glimpse of oneness to the immanent collision of competing needs and perceptions as the limitations of the human heart reveal themselves in the patterns of our conditioning. While it is a humbling and sobering process to integrate awareness of our habitual ways, it is this very awareness that makes possible a conscious realignment of our inner and outer relationships.

From the larger view of the life cycle, pilgrims in the later seasons of life know that it is necessary for those in the summer period to come to fully learn the ropes of the first adulthood. Therefore, this is a time when awareness of Self continues to remain mostly latent. The gradual awakening of our original nature requires a firm establishment and rootedness of our learned, egoic identity within the physical and social fabric of our lives. This is a time for building the foundation of work and new, primary relationships. It is also a time for exercising the powers of physical and cognitive capacities brought to full development in the springtime period. Elder pilgrims know that, until we have been initiated, tested, and fully settled into the adult world, we cannot begin to adequately judge or challenge the foundations of what we have come to perceive as our reality.

Creating the second life platform, we find ourselves faced with the task of crossing the threshold from the buoyant playfulness and imagination of childhood to the weightier, pressure-filled responsibilities and commitments

---

[12] Nagarjuna (1986). *Nāgārjuna: The Philosophy of the Middle Way* (D. Kalupahana, Trans.). State University of New York Press. (Original work published ca. 150 CE)

of adulthood. Preparing to enter the ranks of more experienced pilgrims, we now feel summoned toward the intense gravitational forces that distinguish the adult world from that of the child. We refer to this period as a time of "grounding," of fully entering the physical dimension of being. Grounding is a time of complete immersion into the immanent aspect of life accompanied by an almost total identification with the conditioned self. Embracing the tasks and expectations of adult life makes it possible for us to build a structure that will be able to bear its weight.

As we build the house of adulthood, our readiness and resonance draw us to the Beloved Other as we together begin to create the container within which the roots of our union may grow deeply and solidly. Sacred joining with the Beloved creates a concrete and living tension of opposite energies, containing the whole of universal possibilities and a promise that we have eyes that can see our conditioned patterns where we ourselves are blind. Without the love and mirroring of the other, we are like a ship in a storm without a lighthouse to guide our way. The authentic foundation of our union opens doors to a level of creation that would otherwise be inaccessible. We begin to witness this also in the bonds that we create with our larger work and social worlds. While we develop our individual creative capacities, we are continually reminded of the greater potentialities that are available when souls merge their energies together in a larger synergy.

The expanded field of energy generated when beings unite is like a beacon of light which draws those souls waiting to be welcomed into the world of human life. When we welcome a new life into our hearts, we are entering a pivotal place within the cycle of life that challenges our most engrained patterns and forever changes our relationship to our perception of self and reality. Face-to-face with the gravity of immediate responsibilities, we find that we are no longer the recipient of vital Energies from others; we are now called to become a conduit through which the stream of life circulates to other souls growing within their new physical form. This emergent task invites us to discover the rigors that are necessary to consciously open and *channel* the flow of Essence to provide the food of its energy to others. Without the willingness to consciously bear the weight of intergenerational responsibilities and commitments, ours and the evolution of our human community will not be able to flourish. In the absence of elder pilgrims committed to the challenge of actively nurturing this awareness for the sake of the collective, the full fruition of the cycle of the seasons cannot occur.

The intense inner gravity of this challenging time can produce profound stresses to the body-mind, signaling that a change in our usual homeostasis is occurring. The result of becoming overly identified with the immanent dimension is a constriction of the life force that can leave us gasping as if slowly suffocating from a lack of oxygen. Imbalances arising from an over-alignment with the conditioned aspect of being can have severe emotional and physical repercussions. Dis-ease within the body-mind is a natural effect of prolonged stress caused by a restriction of life energy. Ailments generated by this new dynamic will likely cause us to grasp for relief of our mounting distress. At this juncture, however, it may be difficult for us to comprehend that our suffering is a predictable effect of the overly earthbound conditions inherent to this period of human life. Consequently, we may find ourselves experiencing many dead ends and misdirections as we seek respite from our suffering.

Still bound to the perception that Life Energies lie outside of the boundaries of conscious relationship, we may pursue external methods to alleviate the state of our inner suffering. We have yet to realize that we are attempting to re-establish an experience of inner equilibrium in the face of a shifting tide that has taken us off balance by our over-identification with the preliminary self. We may find a plethora of medicines, substances, and experiences available that provide us with temporary relief from this depletion of life energies. However, the transitory effects of these methods only reinforce the fact that they are conditional and fleeting in their ability to achieve control over our internal balance. If not for our suffering, calling to us to regain a new experience of inner stability, we would likely not become interested enough to begin to awaken to the specific nature of the conditioned bubble of reality in which we find ourselves trapped.

Within the current vernacular, we may begin to view our awakening as a journey of "healing." We may think of it as such because of the tendency to perceive the dis-ease produced by these developmental processes as an illness from which we must attempt to recover. While the preliminary self is indispensable to our ability to organize and modulate life energies, its dominance becomes confining as we slowly sense an opening to a new and different quality of being. We may focus our efforts initially within the borders of the conditioned self as an effort to change or unlearn patterns that we think might be contributing to our inner turmoil. It is also not uncommon for us to attempt to bypass altogether the influences and conditions of our earthbound identity. Many will attempt to board transcendental flights straight to the Source, hoping to circumvent the processes and disciplines that are required to facilitate actual awakening. Many techniques and methods have arisen over the ages to address the Soul's suffering as we, like a salmon swimming upstream to the spawning ground, attempt to regain an experience of inner harmony in the process of re-discovering our origins.

Regardless of the routes taken, a completed journey through the territory of the conditioned self must be made to gain full awareness of our learned patterns of thinking, feeling, and behavior. Without this awareness, the next level of differentiation to a broader, more inclusive re-cognition of Self cannot occur. As we traverse the never-ending pathways and loops through this learned aspect of being, we gradually discover a circular and deterministic topography that only leads back to itself. It is like an eternity of the rolling of a rock up a hill, only to have it roll back down so that we may begin the task over and over again. While seemingly fruitless or meaningless at first glance, the rolling of the rock must occur until we develop awareness of the restrictive "cage" of our conditioning and gradually become ready to release ourselves from the confines of our exclusive alignment with our earthbound identity.

At this point in our journey, we might begin to sense a new threshold that is ours and ours alone to cross. As we approach the beginning of the passage through midlife, we begin to discern the seeming abyss that lies at the precipice of this juncture. We may intuit that we are at the gates of something both familiar and new, a pathway like a birth canal that can feel both dark and ominous. Fearful, we may turn away from the gates that open to this new terrain only to resort to old, familiar ways of negotiating obstacles and challenges. They no longer work for us at this point in time, however, as we are now entering a new season, a new territory, with an unfamiliar landscape that requires opening to a larger and deeper perspective and experience of Self. If we are receptive, more experienced pilgrims may be available to guide our way through. We must be willing, however, to humbly *be in the question*, in a position of surrender to this new phase of human life. For, in this new season of the Soul's voyage, we are on a journey to discover that it is *we* who hold the key to the cage in which we now feel ourselves imprisoned.

Summer // Shemah

By the time I reached adulthood, I felt myself a full member of the human community; I felt connected with others — my parents, my friends, and the human project as a whole. Even though I reached the age of adulthood, I had no idea what it meant to be an adult. I was naively ready to jump headfirst into the sea of life, with no clue as to how vast and deep the ocean can be, how treacherous the tides, currents, and storms can become, and how varied and dangerous its inhabitants were. This was certainly a time of building, of launching my life into an orbit that would support me through my later years. There was plenty of time for the pruning that would come later when it was required that I learn to let go of that which was no longer life-giving or consonant with the vision of my unfolding life.

The bravado that I carried from adolescence served to be a double edge for me. The carefree smiles of my youth were gradually transformed by the realization that I was in deep waters without the yet developed skills to stay afloat in order to find my way toward solid ground. In my attempts to tread the turbulent waters of early adulthood, I was searching for a stable structure that was not only safe and secure but also one that would become a launching pad for the adulthood that I was envisioning.

Looking back upon my 93 years, I find that I am more able to appreciate the weight, the depth, and the breadth of our full immersion into human life. When I think of the Gospel of Thomas teaching "If you bring forth what is within you, what you bring forth will save you; If you do not bring forth what is within you, what you do not bring forth will destroy you," I understand now what this entails and the courage and fortitude that is involved as we risk bringing forward the gifts that are ours alone to manifest. There were many times in my life when I neither had the courage nor understanding of how to bring forward what was within me. I was completely unsure about my capacities to establish enduring connections with others, finding myself caught in the question as to whether I would be able to successfully enter adult life. I searched deeply within myself for a sense of direction, for the courage to learn to become receptive to the guidance that only presents itself in the form of grace. It was within this grace that often comes in moments of perceived helplessness or despair that I miraculously saw a doorway that I previously thought was not open to me. This receptive position became a teaching that helped me to understand that the path ahead was not always an obvious or linear one and that it required an ability to recognize subtleties that lay beyond the surface layers of understanding.

As I look through the rear-view mirror, patterns that were once unintelligible and confusing have gradually become clearer to me. The crystallization of these images has offered a glimpse of my larger path, and from this broader perspective, the parts have begun to make sense. As the pieces came together, I found that I was fascinated by where this all was going. The beauty, the intelligence, not only gave meaning to the dark and oftentimes tragic set of circumstances that surrounded me but also illuminated the depth and significance of who we are in this mystery.

Mine, like the lives of all others, is no mere biography. As I grew into my middle years, I began to see my life as an evolving mystery with new territories to explore and new treasures to uncover. In my earlier years, I did not understand that I was on such a journey. I was engaged in the very difficult task of learning to stand on my own two feet, slowly discovering my worth as a human being and the meaning of my connections with others who shared my path. I didn't know that suffering and confusion were part of the constant reorganizing that comes as one's life unfolds though the lifespan. I was experiencing continually shifting demands that required me to apply everything that I had learned and was learning to adapt to the necessity of creating and sustaining a foundation of my own. It slowly became clear that, until I had completed this task, I had no way to truly begin my life in a way that would allow me to fulfill my destiny as I saw it.

Bringing forward what was within me took on many different meanings and characteristics throughout my life. Prior to midlife, I was deeply involved in the process of building a career and learning how to be a friend, husband, father, and partner to others. While I had many new "choices" before me, they were *not yet my choices*. They were *exercises in choice* to learn to make judgments and to begin the process of taking charge of my life. I had not yet discovered the part of me that was capable of choice, of making decisions that were not enmeshed in the old tapes and motivations of childhood. It would be a considerable amount of time before I could say that the inner Center that I stood on was my own and not simply that which I adopted from my early beginnings. Any openings to deeper realms of Self remained ephemeral and not part of the weighty agenda that tended to focus on more concrete things, such as learning the basics of living on my own, paying the bills, and adhering to the often-cumbersome responsibilities of adult life. But make no mistake about it, this was, at that time, what it meant to bring myself forward.

I had great dreams for my life. My ideals were often frustrated, however, by the immediate realities and challenges that so frequently presented themselves in the process of simply learning how to be an adult. I often wished I could bypass the tasks and stages of my youth so that I could attain some place of wisdom that I know now only comes with the many trials and evolving tasks of life. I must admit that I look back with envy at that youthful time, wishing that I could have enjoyed more the tenderness and vulnerability that was so much a part of entering a new and exciting phase of life. Entering the world, entering my body, living within the structure and the confining limits of slowly developing consciousness was never my strong suit. I wanted to plow right through all the stages of life like when you walk through a labyrinth and wish you could skip all the weaving in and out of the winding, circuitous path and plunge right into the center. I didn't understand then that each part of my life had its own purpose and integrity, and without the solid consolidation of each phase, I was unprepared for the weight of the next, even more challenging set of tasks.

Within what I will call my first adulthood, I was entering a period of life in which the prior roadmap drawn from childhood no longer reflected this new, emerging topography. Not only was this confusing to me, but just when I thought that I had learned to steer clear of the landmines that had so plagued the scenery of my childhood and adolescence, I found myself faced with new ones around which I had no idea how to navigate. Entering uncharted territory, I simultaneously felt a sense of terror and an untested and inflated assumption that I had the self-knowledge to successfully engage this new level of life. This, indeed, was a truly faulty assumption. While the capacities and skills that grew during my early years where necessary for my crossing into adult life, they were in no way sufficient for building and sustaining mature relationships and traversing the hardball world of being a "grown up." These new circumstances required a profound adjustment that challenged the very core of my self-worth and identity, struggles that would plague me through the larger part of my life.

From the distant gaze of old age, I can see more clearly what was not at all evident to me as a young adult. The egocentricity and dependence of youth views others as the source of love and security. I had not yet developed a solid identity of my own, a sense of self that had grown mature and receptive enough to connect with the sustaining love that originated from within. Leaving home was like being unhooked from an invisible emotional lifeline. It was a rude awakening to discover that what was provided for me was not of my making, and that it was now my sole responsibility to create and maintain the connections that had always been so vital to my well-being. New circumstances of life were calling me to transition from a form of relationship built upon the perception that the source of love derives from others to one involving a mutual expression of giving and receiving. I must admit that I was slow to make this transition and to mature the awareness necessary for moving beyond the fears that stifled my development in this area.

Like all human beings, I would not have survived without the love and protection provided by the adults who cared for me. This foundational awareness is often minimized or forgotten when we enter new, primary relationships. The powerful inner thrust I needed to make strides in moving beyond my early dependencies seemed to obscure just how much reassurance I still required to feel that I was standing on secure ground. My early, prolonged isolation as a newborn added an additional fly to the ointment of what was already a loaded equation for me as I was forming new, adult bonds. It takes great inner security to engage in a world of relationships in which little safety can really be provided by others. I did not have this feeling of self-assurance as a young man; I found myself gravitating toward ways of relationship that I hoped would alleviate my fears, as well as reinforce the illusion that some modicum of sanctuary existed for me in the other. I was still looking to others to soothe my anxieties and my fears of loss or annihilation. In exchange, I was willing to imagine myself to be far more loving, giving, and accepting than I actually was. I didn't realize the degree to which my self-deception was restricting my authenticity and freedom as a trade-off for an unobtainable sense of safety that I hoped others would provide.

It has been my experience that the Self that sustains us when love is withdrawn by others, the Self that knows that love is foundational to who we are, appears to come slowly to many of us. Until a palpable experience of this inner core awakens and takes hold within us, I believe that we tend, as I did, to continue our childhood position of approaching adult life as if *others* held the key to our inner experience of love. How could we possibly do it differently? It is all we knew, and our very needs for maturing into adulthood once depended upon it. My experiences in adult life continued to challenge this once useful model of relationship until I was forced to begin to surrender a way of being that was no longer functional. While I am using the word "surrender," that is not how I experienced this collapse of old ways. I would often react to these challenges by descending into despair, initially taking very personally my difficulties in attempting to build a new life of relationships and find a solid footing in the world.

It took me many years to realize the distinction between the nature and meaning of "surrender" and "giving up." With each entry into new, unchartered landscapes, I began to learn to intuit when established ways of engaging life no longer had use or application to new sets of circumstances and challenges. I would become very despondent and withdrawn when faced with failure in my strivings to connect with others, often becoming immobilized by the feeling of hopelessness and defeat that would so powerfully consume my sense of myself. It was not until I experienced a total feeling of letting go that I discovered an inner spaciousness so deep and wide that it began to clue me to the existence of something forgotten, something mystical.

This tender awareness allowed me to regain a sense of hope that all was not lost and to perceive that there was something that existed within me that was timeless and eternal. This was the beginning of the inner formation of what was to become more fully conscious later in my life. When feeling backed into a desperate corner of despair and hopelessness, I was faced with the age-old question posed by Shakespeare of whether "to be or not to be." It was within this, the heaviest of questions, that I was able to sense my calling into life and the realization that I had a desire to Be. Even now, when things are not working for me, I turn consciously to a posture of receptivity, to listen with interest, to observe, and to be in the question of the mysterious process of life as it is unfolding. I have learned that "to be or not to be" is, in each moment, a choice, and to be in a position of surrender does not at all mean to "give up."

I once heard that there are two fundamental kinds of courage: "*the courage to be oneself and the courage to be a part of.*"[13] The growing moments of inner spaciousness that existed beyond my usual sense of self provided me with the courage to move about the world with greater authenticity and to speak my truth from a heart that was slowly learning how to open. I was beginning to sense that I had an inner ground of my own, and I was learning how to stand within it. Developing courage to be myself seemed to go hand in hand with my courage to be a part of the world and others as well. To know that I was learning to withstand the struggles, the closeness, and the distance of relationship allowed me to move about life with greater confidence. My growing comfort and connection with others made more possible my ability to engage in the projects of vocation and, eventually, marriage and family.

Looking back upon the slowly constructed scaffolding that supported my adulthood is like viewing a gradually expanding circle. It began first with me, and then spiraling outward in ever larger diameters, it became spacious and strong enough to hold the weight of others. It was either fear or intuition, but somehow, I sensed in my young adulthood that my own inner foundation was not yet evolved or large enough to include another. I was clearly not yet able to expand my attention beyond a focus on my own needs. For some time, I flirted with relationships, finding that I would enter

---

[13] Tillich, P. (1952). *The Courage to Be.* Yale University Press.

more deeply than my emotional capacities could support. I think I knew intuitively, however, that those souls whom I touched and who touched me would live for a lifetime in my heart. It wasn't until much later that I began to appreciate just how deeply those whom I allowed to penetrate my heart continued to live within me and would become part of the tapestry of who I am.

During that period of my life, my focus became centered on my vocation and building a vehicle for the work that I hoped would support my calling to offer something of value to the world. I didn't understand the significance of what this would entail or where the very wonderful and difficult pathways of this calling would lead. What I did know was that I could not begin to open myself more fully to the world of others until my time as a student and an apprentice was completed. Finishing this piece of development made it possible for me to hold the considerable weight of my emerging adulthood and to begin to turn my attention toward the needs of others who presented themselves in my work and personal life. I have witnessed that those who too quickly attempt to hold the weight of the needs of others before attending to cultivation of their own self-development often find themselves on an unstable and collapsing structure. I think we have all felt compelled to place the "cart before the horse" when it comes to our personal needs and priorities. There are also times when the challenges of life do not allow us the luxury of a healthy balance we would have otherwise sought. I was never good at multi-tasking; I knew I had to be ready and able to hold another within my heart before I was able to stretch myself beyond the comfort zone of established ways of being.

The circle that encompassed who I experienced myself to be was gradually expanding beyond the small center of self. My needs also began to grow past a focus on self-development in a way that opened my heart to a desire to share a mutual path with another. I was making space to receive another who would travel along a road that would broaden and deepen both of our worlds. I was ready for love but had no idea what that really meant. I had only the models from my childhood of what it meant to love and to be loved. I knew that I wanted to be loved, but I had little understanding of what was involved in truly receiving another and remaining open to the many and often misunderstood ways that the gift of love presents itself to us. I was certainly awkward and naive, but I was becoming strong enough to endure the broken heart that may come from risking knowing and to be known by another.

In my youth, my attractions to others were often dominated by strong feelings of physical arousal. These experiences were intoxicatingly wonderful and clearly part of the biology that draws souls together before they really have much of a chance to reflect on their union. While I must admit that I still enjoy these chemical reactions that make my body feel so vital and alive, I do not mistake them at all for the deeper connection that lives beyond the initial flame of attraction and joining. It was not until my midlife that the subtle joys of the heart began to vibrate more intensely than the physiology of my body. I believe that this awareness was born more out of a growing sensibility and appreciation for what is at the center of our bonds with others than just a diminishment of my once powerful hormones. I did not come to this awareness quickly or easily; it has taken the greater part of my life to begin to sort out the complexities of loving myself and others.

I have found that there are two distinct ways of engaging love: love that *is* by choice and love that *is not* by choice. I feel that it is a great human desire to be swept away in the rapture that seems to emerge from an almost divine or mystical place. Eros coursing through our bodies, filling and bursting our hearts open and lifting us beyond the stratosphere to experience a little piece of heaven on earth, who would not want such an encounter? Like a moth to a flame, we not only go willingly, but we also plunge into an ecstatic union with another feeling that we are being touched by something divine and indescribably beautiful. When we are called to this love, our choice is only whether we heed or do not heed the call. And so, this sets up the great confusion of humanity that has daunted the hearts of men and woman for all time.

The old man in me sometimes wants to minimize the importance of this ecstatic doorway that beckons us to open to another struggling human being just like ourselves, cautioning of the sober realities that lie at the heart of a so-called "mature" relationship. Yet, it is within my fondest memories of love's first embrace that I go to this fertile place of re-experiencing the reservoir of love within myself that was first introduced to me through the eyes and the heart of another. For that, I will be eternally grateful. So powerful and intoxicating were those eyes, those lips, the warmth, and beauty of merging energies that I, of course, wanted to return to this well over and over again to drink in the waters of life that flowed so freely in the presence of this magical other.

Like all intoxications, the harsh landing of sobriety and the disappointment of my naive hopes and expectations were never far off. I would eventually begin to wonder who we really were to each other, oftentimes doubtfully questioning what it was that we touched in one another that sparked such a sense of the divine. The flame eventually diminishes, the passions temper, and we find ourselves face-to-face with another struggling, vulnerable human being. The initial experience of calling, of attraction beyond reason and choice, gradually became transformed into a feeling of disillusionment and retraction. If I remained present long enough, it would eventually evolve into a compassionate interest in the life and journey of another imperfect human being like me. For so long, I sat in the question of the very reality of love, thinking of it as an illusion that, in our drunken moments, simply allows us to risk moving beyond our fears of safety to take the leap of faith to join with another. Far from having a complete picture of the nature of loving, it wasn't until I took the conscious risk to *choose* to open my heart to another imperfect human being that I began to understand the relationship between what was chosen and what was beyond choice. What I did sense was that I was being called to expand beyond the small circle of self that was initially constructed to hold one.

Relationship, and eventually marriage, called me to expand beyond myself in ways that I never could have begun to imagine. In order to love another, for love to mature, I realized that I had to stretch beyond any idea I held of what it meant to love or to be loved. As a child, I had learned to feel entitled to love but to be very afraid of its loss. I had not yet discovered what it meant to love without attachment to its return, and how to sustain a heart connection in the presence of feelings that are painfully contrary to those that initially brought us together. My attachment to entitlement and security had to die for me to open to a fuller understanding of love. I had to learn to access something within myself that could endure the times when love felt absent or withdrawn. As my relationships matured, I began to become aware of old ways of being that placed so much expectation on the other for needs that were ultimately not their responsibility nor within their capacity to fulfill. In turn, I was learning not to place unrealistic expectations on myself to fulfill needs that were also beyond my responsibility or capacity. I was learning to become accountable for my emotional life in ways that I could not have in my youth, but I had yet to discover the source of love that lay within that I had so fully attributed to others.

Together with a loving and committed companion, I was taking on the full weight of adulthood and beginning to understand that the joining of two whole worlds makes possible a field of awareness so much larger than the one we create alone. It is an act of grace that two people can open to one another fully enough to include in their mission the well-being and path of the other. When we couple, however, it is initially difficult for us to reconcile between our experiences of the soul and those of long-held childhood patterns. These contrasting expressions of being live side-by-side in all relationships, creating a living tension that continuously calls us into deeper awareness of our early conditioning. Inevitable collisions with *all* parts of self potentially awaken us to ingrained ways of thinking, feeling, and behaving if we engage our journey as a sacred path.

It is the greatest of responsibilities and challenges to hold in our keeping the tender Being of the other and the *process* of their unfinished evolution as they develop. *The fidelity of marriage is, at its best, the disciplined and committed act of loving by consciously holding the heat, the suffering, the beauty, and the growing pains that enable both our and our beloved's lives to transform and mature.* Fortunately, as the expanse of relationship evolves over time from a shallow "puddle" to an infinitely deep "ocean," storms moving in and out gradually transition from violent upsurges to a pattering of droplets as the sea of respect, trust, loyalty, and discernment of priorities grows increasingly spacious. *It took me some time to realize that a truly sacred human-to-human marriage is an outer - reflection of the irreversible commitment one holds to the evolution of their deepest, inner spiritual path.*

To view my life through the eyes of a loving other enabled the humility to see myself more clearly and to learn to accept within myself what I had previously experienced as intolerable. So much of the energy that I placed in preparing to enter life, to feel myself worthy and capable of love, was now able to transform into the larger project of building a life in which I was no longer the central character. This was a strange transition for me in that it was I who was now called to provide and maintain the ground upon which other beings could grow and flourish. I was never quite sure that I was cut out for such a considerable task, but I engaged in what I saw as my responsibilities seriously and wholeheartedly. I had entered life fully, or so I thought. My life was about to change drastically, and forever.

On the cusp of midlife and while just beginning to find my sea legs as an adult, my father became suddenly and gravely ill. I had experienced loss before and believed that I had some intimate knowledge of grief. I was slow to realize, however, just how great the dimensions of the human soul really are. Like many young people who have only scratched the surface of their lives, I, too, believed I had experienced a reality beyond an outward experience of things. Awakening to the unexplored depths of feeling comes unexpectedly and harshly to those of us who think we have some idea about what awaits us when the hand of life pulls us into the deepest waters of the heart. I was no different. I could not have conceived what was about to open as the hand of death came knocking upon the door that stands between the known and the unknown.

My father's death followed soon after his illness. It was the end of a time in which I felt that I could still be carried by another. His loss was like the skin being peeled off the outer layer of my body, exposing a raw, unfinished human being to the elements of life of which my father was, for so long, a buffer. Memories cycled before my eyes as I re-experienced the primal textures of the connection that brought me so close to his heart. I had not seen nor fully appreciated the degree to which he lived within me and comforted my tender soul as I was growing into manhood. He will always live within me, yet experiencing the tearing away of his human presence felt like something precious within me had died as well. I had not yet known this level of death within myself, or the new landscapes of awareness it would begin to reveal. I felt myself on the precipice of a cliff, looking out upon a vast expanse with little sense of just how deep, how treacherous, and how wondrous was the vista that had been shielded from my view for all these years.

My grief and ability to feel what extended far beyond my usual sense of experience was a terrifying revelation to me. It would be many years before I would begin to comprehend the meaning of this rupture in the egg of my identity and to understand the toehold it had on the organization and re-organization of my inner sense of self. I was gradually being "sucked" through the crack in the vessel that could no longer contain what was moving and emerging within me, as if entering a very long and dark birth canal after the water had broken. Struggling to re-emerge from the shadowy depths and the loneliness of loss that followed this seminal event in my life, I could not even begin to fathom the degree to which everything was changing and would continue to re-organize until I was on the other side of this protracted, dark, and transfiguring experience of transition. Feeling myself in an abyss beyond description, my instinctive reaction was to reach back for familiar ways or to find strategies to attenuate the intense anxiety that continued to emerge as I fell through the disorienting darkness. I was fortunate, at that time, to have a mentor who would guide by encouraging me to remain present to the experience of pervasive darkness and unknowing. It was not until many years later, and after his death, that I began to understand what he meant in his insistence that the light would be revealed as I continued to descend deeper into the darkness.[14]

The not yet solid structure of my life was expanding beyond two and growing to welcome a new life and another radical change in the ever-shrinking importance of my self. My energies were being called upon to give of myself on so many levels while I was also struggling to just stay composed as I was learning to walk within the shadows of discarded feelings and memories yet to be claimed. I felt like I was drowning in the

---

[14] Mentor referred to is Fr. Dunstan Morrissey, OSB (1923-2009).

deep waters of all that terrified or overwhelmed me. My wife would wisely say to me, "You need to learn how to relax and to *breathe underwater*." Suffocating, my energies depleted, just like my struggle to find the light within the darkness; I did not know how to breathe underwater either.

I was still operating within the old paradigm, reaching to others for the oxygen of love to ease the crushing feeling within my chest. I saw no way out. I felt like I was dying from within, helpless and without control of the soothing I was seeking to ease my suffering. Proud and confused, I had come to the end of the road of my ability to manage my energies as I had in my youth and young adulthood. I had no more inner resources to offer my wife, my children, or myself. I was about to learn about something that would begin to restore memories long forgotten. But first, I had to admit that the demands for what was required of me at this time in my life had now exceeded my usual abilities to meet them.

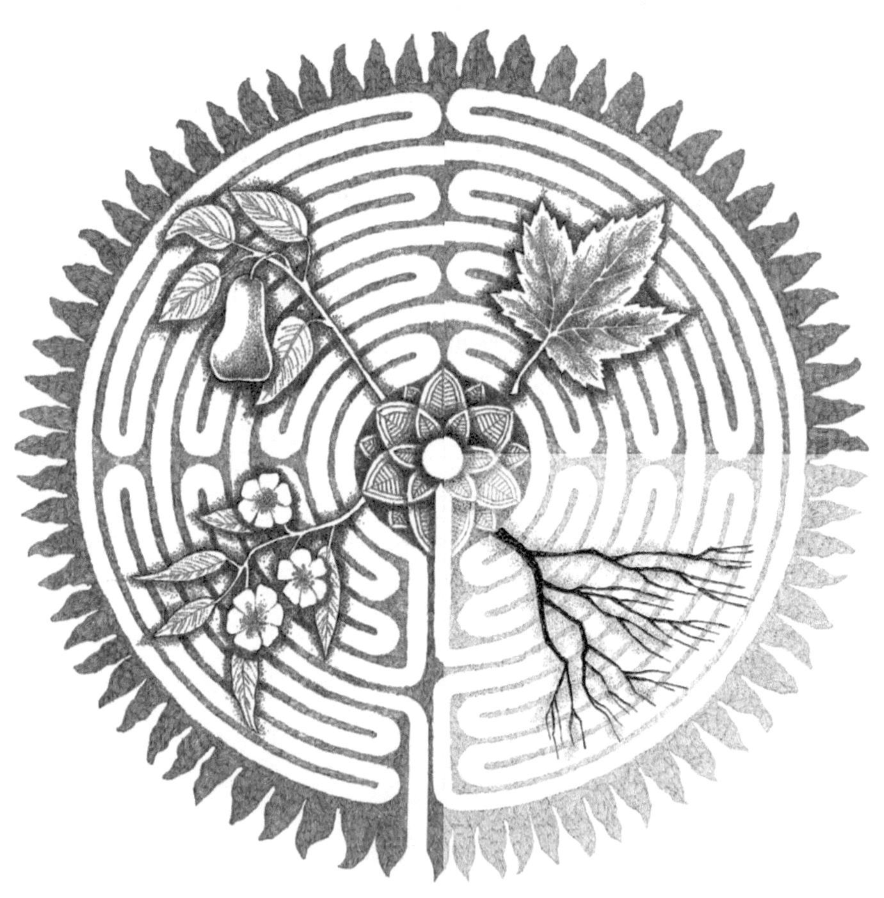

FALL

God sends some persons into the darkness so he can release someone who is in chains.

— Edith Stein

Shemah (1967)

I did not fully understand the master's request that I succeed him, even though I had agreed. It was not long, however, before in-sight came, unbuffered by a painfully intimate embrace with death. It was 1967. Deeply entrenched in an unpopular war in Vietnam, the country was exploding with cultural change and growing pains from within. My own growing pains had not ceased and were certainly a mirror of the times. One stormy night, the wind gusts furiously shaking the trees at the torrential sky outside my office window, I was startled by the sudden ringing of the phone at my desk in my home library. "You need to come home immediately," my mother announced, grief and panic filling her voice as I sensed tears rolling down her cheeks. "Your father had a serious stroke; he was taken to a nearby hospital." My heart sank into my stomach as I contemplated his loss, rushing to pack my suitcase.

He died three days later. Still in shock, I attempted to comfort my mother as we prepared for his memorial. My heart was torn open, heavy, as his loss sank to the soul. I will never forget his peaceful countenance as he took his last breath, life voiding from his fragile body. Flashes of father and son slid one over the over before my eyes, like a View-Master slide projection of our many precious moments together. Circles under my eyes grew and sank deeper as a pervasive sadness penetrated the cells of my body. His loss tore away any remains of childhood and thrust me again into the fathomless dark night. "How could I imagine life without him?" I questioned. Emptied and stripped down, I pined to myself, "I miss you dad." Days later, thinking of the beautiful man as a mound of ashes in the stately urn sitting on my mother's nightstand, sleep would not come. Tossing in my bed in the early AM hours, an encounter altered my life forever.

> *I suddenly was sitting next to my dad in a space unlike anything I had known before, his arm around my shoulder in a loving embrace. "I tried so hard to hold on, but it was like being encased in cement," he communicated. "I couldn't move or speak. I wanted to stay for you and your mother, but my body wouldn't work. So, I finally let go of this shell that I couldn't hold onto any longer. I love you, son. I love you very much," he said. I replied, "I love you, dad."*

Morning light filtered through the curtains, awakening me and breaking our moment together in this in-between space. "I spent the entire night with my father!" I exclaimed to my wife, stunned by this very tangible visitation. "This was NOT one of those dreams we have to process our grief; he came to say goodbye for now and to show me that death is just a transition from the physical body." For the first time, I felt a first-hand connection to "the other side," to the ancestors, and to the true source of life.

The Self was no longer a concept or theoretical construct to me. It was beginning to breathe into renewed life, refreshed in living connection to what once had been invisible to me but now radiated from my depths. The light that Cornelius revealed to me was the light I was now experiencing consciously within. Now that I was mature enough spiritually that the outer shell of identity could be released, he was showing me a level of my Self that I had been unprepared to apprehend in my youth when I clearly needed to experience him as "other." This awakening eventually centered me in the flame of my own authentic core where I finally understood: The master was not asking me to become him; he was asking me to choose to become my Self.

Fall // Author

Having crossed the threshold of midlife, I am entranced by the nature of this transition from one territory to another and what it means to be in the question, in surrender. I, too, have often felt the constriction that comes from too much to give and not enough energy to give it. As I have grown older, I have wondered just how one stretches to give as the demands of life ask increasingly more from us as parents, partners, and members of the larger community. Shemah's discourse opens for me the mystery of how we come to recognize the Essence, the Source of life, and begin to realize that it flows within us as it does within everyone and everything. The process of discernment, the task of distinguishing between that which is conditioned and that which is of our true nature, appears to have the potential of unfolding slowly as we navigate through midlife. There are clearly no answers at this juncture. There is only the recognition that what was required of us to navigate through the first half of life must take a back seat to what is emerging in the second half. This transition seems almost like the unsettled weather, the changing of patterns, as we come to the equinox that separates the seasons with their own unique qualities, activities, and temperatures.

Fall // Cornelius

As we approach the middle of our lives, we find ourselves at a critical nexus in which our conditioned identity begins to slowly give way to larger, vital energies. By this time, we will have likely become mothers and fathers, leaders, masters of our trades, and creators of forms that pervade the physical and social landscape of our communities. We may have brought to full fruition our physical and intellectual talents as an expression of skills and attributes developed from our early training. We might also have become fully settled into our identification with our traits and characteristics and the social realities in which we are immersed. Along with the now visible aging of our bodies, we may notice, however, a gradual loss of meaning and interest in those things that before had sparked our desire. Moving further into the chasm of midlife, we begin to discover that what we have become and are becoming can no longer be contained within the confining shell of the increasingly tenuous preliminary identity.

From the moment of birth, while establishing the foundations of our conditioned skills and identity, the gestation of the "spiritual fetus" was maturing side by side with our evolving sense of self. While usually dormant and only gradually available to awareness during the spring and summer periods of life, our Essential nature has always provided the "real" inner holding space for us while the physical body and social identity were taking form. For those who choose life circumstances that produce early disruptions of development, we may precociously become witness to these naturally latent dimensions because of early fissures in the vessel of the developing ego identity. Conditions perceived as disability, disease, or trauma are highly transformative in their capacities to enhance awareness of human vulnerability and the tenderness of the heart. Choices to live within challenging circumstances such as these that might, otherwise, be disparaged from a narrow point of reference are, paradoxically, highly sought after by those seeking to broaden their creative repertoire. While potentially a source of immense suffering, these experiences can be a powerful catalyst to the blossoming of unique and valuable forms of awareness. When the usual formation of the body or brain is interrupted during sequences of development, differing inner balances alter the organization of our relationship to Essence in ways that can only occur under these specific conditions. Each modification of the dynamic of these dual aspects of S/self provides a diversity of angles through which the lens of life might be viewed and experienced. Suffering that results from the adversities that these heroic life choices bring can certainly be unremitting and confusing. Yet, there is nothing that delivers us closer to the heart of our authentic core than those experiences that quicken our awareness and call us into deeper contact with the Source of being.

There is no right way or wrong way to develop in relationship to the tension of these opposites, as each unique perspective offers the very experiences that we choose to live within and through for our evolution. Nonetheless, new patterns that coalesce in the fall, midlife period tend to reflect a predictable recalibration of relationship between early conditioning and our emerging Self. This transition offers an opportunity to re-align these fundamental inner relationships, allowing for a more complete, conscious expression of the dual components necessary for higher creation.

Full adulthood requires an emergent attention to the development, maturation, and wellbeing of others, as well as a heightened awareness of our own emotional and physical needs. When we remain overly identified with the preliminary self, the demand for life energy, for ourselves and for others, begins to far outweigh the supply. The constricted flow of energy caused by old, unconscious ways of being consequently sets in motion a downward spiral of physical and emotional well-being as we struggle to adapt to the changing inner and outer demands of adulthood. It is natural for us to call upon earlier developed strategies as we attempt to reach for known forms and methods of coping to ease our suffering. We have yet to realize that our suffering is being generated by encounters with once dormant awareness that is now beginning to expand and breakthrough the familiar, secure, and sheltering egg of our conditioning.

Tectonic pressures caused by emerging consciousness begin to fragment early constructions of established identity. This fracturing also includes the second platform that we have so diligently created within the summer period of our lives. The suffocating experience produced by the confining shell of the conditioned self may be experienced more like a cage than a protective womb that hothouses our True Nature until we are ready for its re-emergence. Unknowingly, this encounter with the "larger" Self is more like a second birth which is delivering us into a new topography of life for which no prior template or map exists.

We must remember that the *First Birth* marks the emergence of the ego-self as a differentiated extension of the Ground of Being, the larger Self, and functions as the primary center of conscious experience during the first half of life. The ego as an *autonomous* pole of consciousness creates the illusion of duality, a psychological environment of opposites, and functions as a conduit and metabolizing agent for manifesting Self-awareness. In other words, the stable ego, as a *separate psychic system*, makes it possible for the Self to observe and become increasingly conscious of itself.[15]

The *Second Birth*, on the other hand, involves a gradual re-union of the now cohesive and stable ego-self with the larger Source of Being. *Reunion must not be confused with identification, however, as identification with the boundless, transcendent Oneness is fraught with the inflation of confusing ourselves with the Source itself. Therefore, differentiation of our relationship to the immanent and transcendent levels of Self must occur if we are to keep the psyche in proper balance and maintain our connection to the Divine Essence without losing our footing in everyday human existence (e.g., in Hinduism, there are the Atman and the Brahman; in Judaism, there are Eloheinu and Adonai; and, in Christianity, there are the Son and the Father as the personal and transcendent faces of God). Also, while our link to transcendent, Essential Being is never broken, this rebirth to a conscious, sustainable, and grounded experience of Self involves recentering, not to the transcendent, but to the immanent, imperishable personal Self; this represents a transition of our relationship to Self from the immanent background (which is unconscious) to the ever-integrating foreground of awareness (which is conscious).*

This return to Self is not a diminishment of the importance of the ego as a *servant*, however, or its necessity in effectively navigating the physical dimension. Rather, the new role of the ego-self involves a *conscious subordination*[16] from that of primary identity to a receptive ambassador of the Self. Gradual emergence from the background of consciousness enables the *imperishable* personal Self (often referred to as Soul) to now take an increasingly primary role in informing and guiding awareness — while

---

[15] Neumann, E. (1949). *The Origins and History of Consciousness*, originally published in German as *Ursprungsgeschichte des Bewusstseins* by Rascher Verlag, Zürich.

[16] Shany, L., Neumann, E. (2025). *The Theory*. Chiron Publications.

the ego-self continues to assert its indispensable mastery as an "organ" of consciousness by mediating, receiving, assimilating, and synthesizing this larger awareness so that we may navigate the many levels of human existence and accomplish the developmental tasks of the second half of life.

The patterns and resonance of the preliminary identity, the ego-self, however, likely reflect the only reality of which we have become aware since we entered the physical dimension. We may begin to realize that we have reached the end of a known territory within the boundaries of established patterns of thinking, feeling, and behaving. As we expand beyond familiar landscapes of the psyche, new, emerging awareness can bring us into sober contact with, once repressed, shadow elements of our inner life. Encountering these exiles of the psyche can become a terrifying challenge to the secure structure of the life that we have worked so industriously to create. Suffering, occurring as we begin our descent through the dark corridors of the birth canal of midlife, can cause us to brace and tighten our grip further as we furiously attempt to dig deeper in the dry midlife soil where life was once so fertile.

Resistance to birthing this new experience of Self only serves to further entrap us in the dark, protective womb of the preliminary identity. This is often experienced as a time of emergence(y), in which the restriction of expanding awareness can result in serious imbalances within the physical and emotional systems of the organism. Stresses produced by this disequilibrium, this resistance, can become emotionally and physically debilitating, particularly in locations of the body-mind where energies are most constricted. It is not unusual or inappropriate to seek assistance to alleviate suffering that naturally emerges with awareness that has been segregated from our hearts for a lifetime. Our initial experience of this shifting ground may not be one of birth but, rather, a feeling that the life within which we have been so firmly rooted and to which we so steadfastly cling is dying and shattering into a million pieces around us.

Severe stresses produced by the labor-pains of the death and re-birth of our shifting center can bring us to a position of surrender unlike any we have ever known before. The dissolution of our identification with the preliminary self is like the breaking of the heart of our earlier hopes and aspirations. It is often accompanied by the experience of *mortification* that leads not to the building of new structures but, rather, to the gradual release or death of forms and patterns no longer useful in navigating within these next territories of being. As we enter each new season, we slowly discover that we cannot effectively bring our earlier identifications with us. We come to realize that, like a turning wheel, the river of life does not traverse the same terrain twice.

Depleted, despondent, and desperate, we may continue to drill within the dry wells of earlier established ways of being. We might search frantically for every possible way to return to previous life structures that we believe held for us experiences of security and stability. We may even resort to dangerous and destructive ways of coping, of numbing or medicating our internal feelings of despair and disorientation as we cross the chasm between the known and unknown. Without guidance, we may become lost in a fathomless abyss from which we find little hope of light at the end of the tunnel. At these times, it is not unusual to attempt to return to earlier dependencies and strategies that allowed us to adapt to the constraints of life within the conditioned bubble of reality.

With care and direction from more experienced pilgrims, we can make the necessary descent though the corridors of the birth canal as we begin to peel away surface layers and re-integrate dis-membered and discarded parts that had been cast out of our conception of self long ago. It is a rare pilgrim who can make it through to the other side of this "dark night of the soul" without the guidance of compassionate midwives who themselves have become firmly rooted in the process of re-membering who they are. Those who are decisively aligned with the path of Self-discovery naturally offer a *holding space* for us to open to and embrace the unknown and challenging dimensions of being that lie beyond the shore of who we have believed ourselves to be.

An inability to return to the once protective shelter of the preliminary self compels us to surrender our grasping and makes possible the re-positioning necessary for receiving a new influx of vital energy. We may become more aware of the ways in which these life energies are available to us as an experience of light fills the darkness of our long journey of surrender and release. We may also begin to observe the ways in which we consciously or unconsciously resist or allow the flow of Essential Energy through the various centers of our organism. What once involved (in the spring and summer) a *horizontal* extension from one human being to another now includes a more conscious, *vertical* inner connection from ego to Self. This transition to include vertical relationship is not intuitive by nature, given that we are so steeped in the practice of horizontal ways of being in which the ego survives childhood and early adulthood by relying on human-to-human connection as the primary source of sustenance.

Birthing into new consciousness, however, is not meant to be an escape or release from the invaluable foundations of our earlier conditioning; it is meant to build upon the ground that has enabled this new awareness to continue to expand. It also allows us to become increasingly attentive to the specific ways we modulate and focus the energies of the life force. The gathering consciousness that opens us to realities beyond our initially constructed ideas about who we are consequently summons a new, major developmental process. *Development is no longer driven by the experience of separation from the Ground of Being as it had been in the springtime, or from the Primal Others (nuclear family) as it had been in the summer period; it now, in fall, becomes characterized by separation or differentiation from our earlier, conditioned identity formation.* The perspective created by continued expansion beyond earlier modes of development makes possible a more conscious examination of the basis of our patterns of thinking and feeling. It also sheds light on the ways in which these patterns have shaped the foundations of what we have come to perceive as our reality.

Each step toward conscious re-centering of Self makes possible the detachment necessary from our conditioning to critically examine the basis of how we perceive the world around us. We will not be able to release ourselves from attachment to our first adult identity until we are able to open ever more fully to what lives at our authentic core. *The fall period represents a dramatic shift from an "extroverted" identification with the "outer," physical dimension, to a more "introverted" interest and engagement with the "inner" life of the Self.* A more refined awareness of established patterns of thinking, feeling, and behavior enables us to distinguish between that which is conditioned and that which arises from our Essential depths. Growing discernment of the distinctive resonances of these differing levels of S/self makes possible a slow repositioning that leads to a newly re-organized center of consciousness. To be able to eventually say to ourselves and know, "This is who I am," is the key that opens the gates to a larger view of the purpose and meaning of our lives.

As the soul journeys further into the fall period of life, these movements represent the dusk of the primacy of the conditioned self and the dawn of the primacy of the previously dormant Essential Self. The shifting poles of our relationship to the dual centers of consciousness can be quite disorienting as we attempt to gain footing within these new dynamics of internal balance and organization. As we release from the second platform, it is not unusual to continue to experience a compulsion to repeat familiar patterns of thinking that underlie earlier attachments. We may also struggle to maintain traction as we open increasingly to the subtle qualities of Self.

There are many stories and examples in human history when death comes to one way of being as we begin to open to another way. There are parables of exodus, of wandering in the forest or the desert, during which old patterns are released without a clear vision or bridge to the next way life. We may wander in these gap spaces for considerable periods of time without a map to orient us or guides to direct us. While not providing the usual geography with which we might be accustomed, these gap or "bardo" spaces are fertile periods in which new creation might be born from the chaos of possibility. We will find ourselves in between life structures, one confining and outgrown and one expansive and beyond our comprehension. This new formation, however, must *not* be born from the ego but from a nascent Self that we are only beginning to sense, a new center of being that must grow in connection and experience for us to make our way through the gap-space from enslavement to greater freedom.

Experience with the resonance of the Source of life is necessary to know its unique vibrational qualities more fully. The emerging memory of our interminable connection to Self allows its energy to penetrate us more completely. Re-awakening to our origins in love opens us as well to awe and wonder as we glimpse the great abundance and variety of possibilities present within creation. A palpable sense of being fully alive within a complex, wondrous, expansive, and loving universe fills us with the joy of greater union as growing awareness reveals the reality of our connection to everything and everyone. We may feel as though a "prodigal son" or daughter returning home from a long excursion through the dense wilderness of the soul.

This ecstatic opening after a lifetime of dedication to the preliminary self can create another kind of imbalance, one in which identity shifts in the opposite direction toward an ungrounded, expansive, and inflated experience. The swinging of the pendulum to the other extreme may be a necessary part of beginning to come to know the boundlessness of our True Nature. Until we become well acquainted with this larger experience of who we are, we may not be able to begin the development of the third platform. The third, fall platform involves the deepening, integrative process of what has been referred to as individuation.[17] Individuation requires an increasing ability to discern, consciously align with, and birth into human life the all-encompassing ground of the Authentic Self, which includes all polarities (e.g., good and evil) and disowned shadow elements. This platform is built upon the question and response to: "Who am I, really, and what does it feel like to be *undivided* within and to welcome home all dimensions of being, particularly those disowned and wounded places that the smaller self could not presence or embrace?"

Until we are attuned to the *felt* memory of who we are, we cannot develop volitional control of the vibrational states generated by consciousness. The journey of re-membering is a process of receptivity and conscious re-integration of dormant and discarded aspects of being. Felt re-cognition of the signature of our original resonance makes it possible for us to know, to experience, the qualitative differences between the immanent, *imperishable personal spirit*[18] (Self) and learned characteristics that are reflective of our early conditioning. This level of observation helps us to see our conditioning for what it is: nothing more than organized patterns of thought, emotion, and behavior stemming from life experiences and requirements for survival and adaptation. We become aware that these

---

[17] Jung, C.G. (1928). "The Relations between the Ego and the Unconscious" (R.F.C. Hull trans.). In G. Adler, M. Fordham & H. Read (Eds.), *The Collected Works of C.G. Jung,* volume 7: "Two Essays on Analytical Psychology" (p. 267). Princeton University Press.

[18] Kalsched, D. (2013). *Trauma and the Soul.* Routledge.

tendencies are no more real or true than the experiences from which they were shaped.

It is particularly important at this juncture that our expansion remains anchored as we maintain our footing within the temporal dimension. The "grounding" of the summer period provides the mooring necessary for us to welcome and embrace our shifting *center* of self without losing traction in daily life. Devaluation of the material can also present a risk to our balanced development as encounters with our True Nature begin to inform our sense of s/Self. We are not able to create and flourish without full utilization of the skills and capacities developed during the spring and summer periods. We must be careful not to throw the "baby" of the ego identity out with the "bathwater" of its transition into a new role as conduit of the Larger Self. An imbalance, caused by the complete *dis-identification* of the ego-self and an *over-identification* with the Source of Being, can result in inflation and a vulnerability to be overtaken by the powerful grip of primitive, archetypal forces that may interrupt and diminish the higher creative potential that we have come into human life to fulfill.

A great thinker observed that the human personality has an innate tendency to strive toward balance and wholeness during the second half of life. He referred to this propensity for harmonizing the inner and outer worlds of experience as "centroversion."[19] The natural repositioning that is possible for the Soul during midlife holds the potential for reestablishing a new *center of gravity*, a "middle way," between the conscious self and the boundless dimensions of the Source of Being (see image below). This axial centering provides a conduit to a *larger field of energy (Self)* (see image below) and the internal balance necessary for the ego to assimilate and differentiate emerging consciousness. The newly established dynamic

---

[19] Neumann, E. (1949). *The Origins and History of Consciousness*, originally published in German as *Ursprungsgeschichte des Bewusstseins* by Rascher Verlag, Zürich.

tension of the ego – Self axis also acts as a catalyst for an alchemical process that encourages psychic plasticity and fuels the transformative energies of expanding awareness. This union of opposites functions organically to open a portal to a *transcendent*[20] and continually enlarging terrain of consciousness. Without connection to the deep spiritual roots intrinsic to our Center of Being, however, we will not have the emotional capacity necessary to re-integrate and to compassionately embrace fragmented, exiled, and abandoned parts of Self.

The enlargement of consciousness allows us the inner spaciousness and perspective to view the basis of our thoughts and feelings with greater objectivity, a perspective that helps us to more fully appreciate the purpose of the platforms that were created for us to achieve this level of development. The process of re-membering also elicits renewed reflections on the past that can bring about a clearer understanding of the specific ways in which our life has unfolded. This involves not just greater awareness regarding the enduring and repeated patterns formed in earlier life, but also an emergent ability to begin to put together the puzzle pieces of life into new images of meaning. We may notice that each thread of life, though seemingly unconnected when viewed individually, appears to reveal discernible patterns when viewed as a part of the greater whole. As the "sacred text" of life begins to reveal itself, it further affirms that we are never abandoned or alone on our journey and that we always have been held in the loving hands of the Source of life.

Healthy development lays down the progressive physical, psychological, and spiritual foundations necessary for the effective organization and modulation of life force energies. The ability to sustain balanced awareness of both conditioned and unconditioned centers of consciousness creates an

---

[20] Jung, C.G. (1957). *The Transcendent Function* (A.R. Pope, Trans). Zurich Students' Association, C.G. Jung Institute (pp. 23, 55).

internal harmony that allows the flow of life energy to expand and contract more intentionally. Conscious relationship with the multiple dimensions of s/Self broadens awareness of the vibrational qualities that live within us. The intentionality that flows from this emerging awareness directs and shapes the energy that resonates from all corners of being. Therefore, when the many levels of psyche function in harmony, possibilities of higher creations are born. As citizens of both the physical and non-physical, *we again become aware of the great import of the forms we are responsible for bringing into existence with every thought, word, and deed,* as well as the ones that arise spontaneously from our depths and call us to enter life in ways that cannot be anticipated.

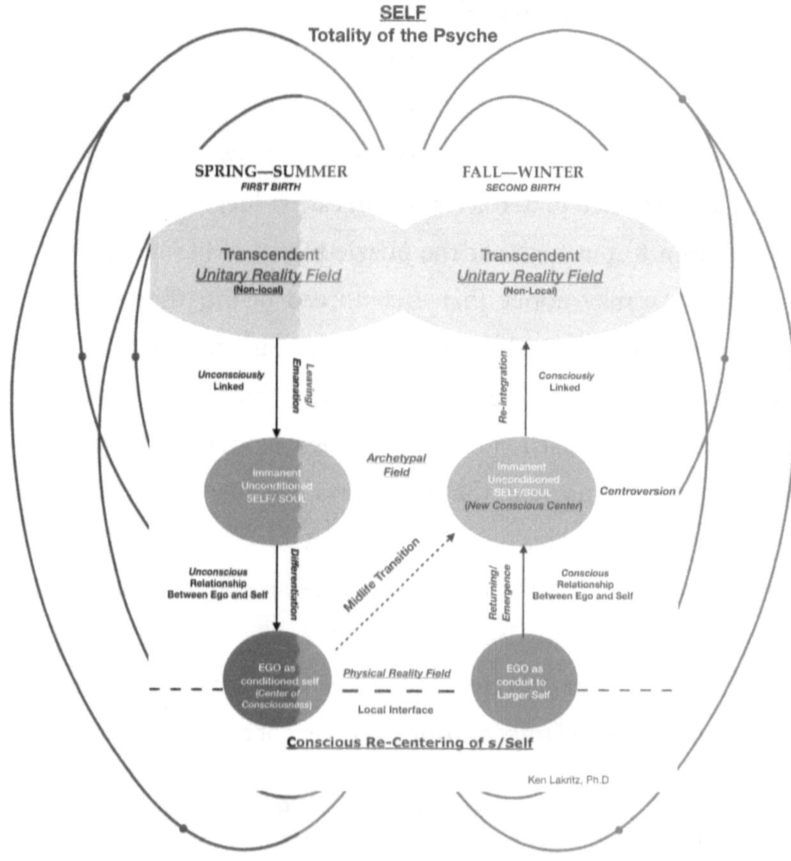

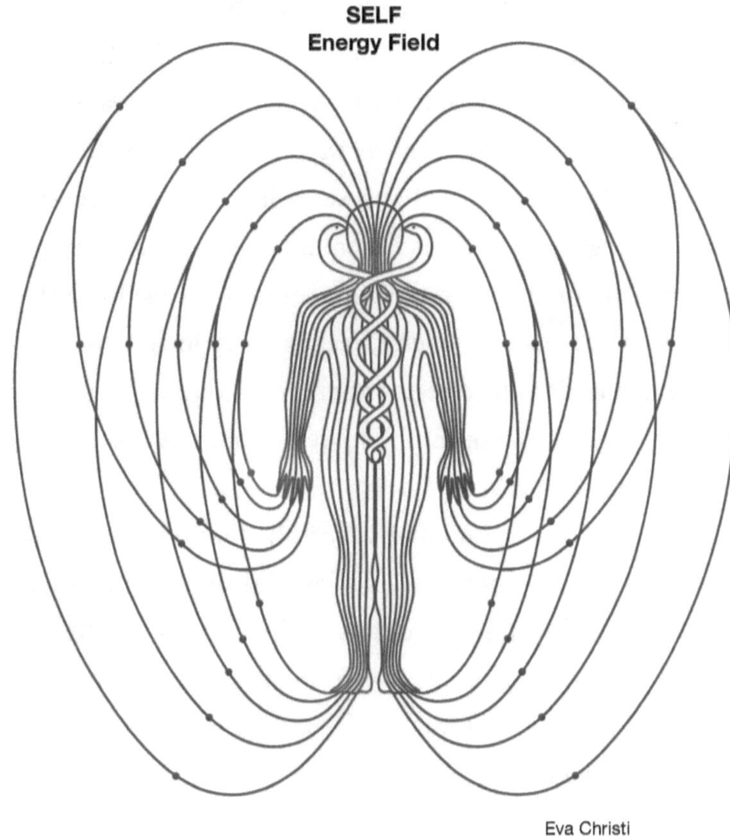

Eva Christi

Fall // Shemah

As I entered the middle years of my life, I remember experiencing the weight of increasing responsibilities that were often accompanied by an unloving inner dialogue that crippled my ability to fulfill them. This was a time of walking in the valley of the shadows, of immersion into the overwhelming tensions between that which had so deeply shaped my character and that which was emerging from the primordial depths of the unknown. I walked the dark corridors of this passage for some time, unclear about what was dying and what was being born. It was the pressing weight on my heart that moved me forward through a territory in which everything that I believed myself to be was being called into question, and everything I thought and felt was becoming open to closer examination. The amplification of memory at this time was a two-edged sword: on one hand, it provided access to thoughts, feelings, and images that I thought had been long buried in the recesses of my consciousness; on the other, it made inescapable my relationship to myself in both its life affirming and life denying forms.

I was truly in the primordial labyrinth, finding myself searching for doorways among minotaurs, gargoyles, and the trolls that guard the entrances that lead beyond the borders of the familiar. Wading through the swamp of all that I had internalized from my parents, from my cohorts, from society over a lifetime, I was able to begin to glimpse those elements of life that I had taken so deeply into myself that they had come to define me from within. Like a fish in water, I had become one with the pond that provided the sustenance for my eventual capacity to grow beyond it. I had yet to appreciate, however, what was involved in moving beyond the identifications that so powerfully shaped my attitudes and defined my relationship to myself. For one as impetuous as me, the dark birth canal in which I found myself was long and filled with painful struggle.

I felt pulled between two opposing experiences of S/self, one calling me forward on faith from a subtle undefined place within, and one refusing to release its grip until I had completed the complicated task of discerning one from the other. Torn between heaven and earth and plagued by the ghosts of those unwanted, unloved parts of myself that I had usually so successfully relinquished from my awareness, I found myself unable to employ typical compensations to shield me from experiencing the pain that lay beneath. I was raw, lying face down in the muddy waters of the debris of thoughts and feelings that had cycled consciously and unconsciously through my awareness since childhood. No longer unconscious, they were there for display, intensified and reified in ways that made them more immediately palpable, accessible, and painful. I was not clear of the purpose of such an exercise in suffering as I wallowed in feelings of regret, self-disappointment, grief, and deep perceptions of inadequacy. I was clearly at the precipice of something for which I had no prior roadmap, and something for which my previous coping strategies were no longer supportive.

Admitting to myself that I was helpless in navigating my predicament, I found myself able to rediscover a forgotten position of surrender and a willingness to reach out for assistance. I had never been one much inclined to pray or ask for outside support, but at that time, I prayed for help. It was as if I were reaching beyond myself with the hope that someone or something would reach back to soothe my despair and feeling of impotence. Unknowingly, I was approaching the end of the birth canal, crowning into a new, larger experience of life waiting for me to have the humility and the courage to simply reach beyond the self-contained world that had carried me to this moment. I reached my hand across the boundary of what I knew toward something, or someone, beyond the realm of anything I could explain in words. It was as if a crack in the egg of my experience of self, my suffering, began to form, eventually breaking open further, allowing new energy to trickle in from what had unknowingly been a well cloistered experience of Self. To my surprise, what entered were experiences of pure love, kindness, and compassion of a sort I had never experienced before. Juxtaposed with my lifelong patterns of self-perception was now a new element, one which not only greatly eased my suffering, but also revealed to me a contrasting facet of experience which began to challenge the very basis of who and what I thought myself to be.

Prior to these moments that forever shifted and reorganized my perception of my place within the universe, I had an inflated view of my own importance in the larger scheme of my own life and that of others. Overwhelmed and deeply humbled, I began to behold the vastness that lay outside of the known boundaries of my small self, and certainly beyond the reaches of any consensual reality. For the first time in my memory, *I could plainly see that I was not the center of all things important but that, indeed, my Center was the origin of all things of importance.* Loving energies gradually flowed from some mysterious place within, and never had I experienced my self as so inconsequential as I had within the grandness of this new reality I felt overwhelmingly honored to glimpse. My suffering abating, I continued to feel as if I were becoming slowly released from the confines of an identity that was not only strangling my energies but also was preventing me from experiencing something larger and more real that would enable me to begin to engage my life more fully.

Taking small steps into an expanded awareness of life that I was just discovering, I found that I was tapping into a source of energy that did not have the same limits as that which I was attempting to manage within my smaller universe of self. The developmental pressures that were opening my horizons eventually pushed me to expand beyond the foundation that can hold only two and three. Standing upon the growing concentric circles that reflected my enlarging experience, my perspective was expanding beyond the narrow perceptions that defined my previous experience of self. This fish was now jumping into a bigger pond that was providing a new vantage point from which to see more clearly the nature of the environment in which I was incubated and immersed for so long.

As with all sequences of development, we often believe that we are much further along the path than we actually are; we do not appreciate the myriad dimensions of knowing that lies perpetually beneath, above, and around our awareness. While I had reached a point where I was beginning to feel the chains of my previous reality loosen their grip, I was far from out of the woods or to the next shore where I would be able to begin to taste the fruits of remembering who I was. The broadening view that was expanding was by no means a large leap into new consciousness, but it did provide a curiosity about the path ahead and an edge of clarity that had not existed before. I knew that there was no turning back to the confining cage of the smaller self that had carried me through my childhood and earlier adulthood. Reversing course would mean ignoring the lessons that had brought me to my knees and allowed me to begin to see just how little I knew about myself and the vast dimensions of life around me.

My need to feel important, to believe that I had the slightest grasp on the workings of myself and the so-called "reality" that I was navigating, became a great impediment to my ability to see beyond my fragile need for a secure sense of myself. It was, ultimately, the love of my wife, my family, my friends, and the compassion that began trickling in from beyond known borders that filled me enough to begin to become willing to look within shadows that were previously avoided and left unattended. Without their love, I would certainly not have had the courage to withstand the needed mirroring that allowed me to become a receptive witness to my own self-imposed darkness and suffering. I was fortunate to have attention brought to blind spots that obscured the very tendencies that most constrained and crippled my deeper self-expression. I am grateful to have others in my life who loved me enough to risk lighting a lamp to these habits of thought, feeling, and behavior that I was either incapable or averse to seeing. Compassionate witnessing by others made it possible for me to begin to discern my native gifts from the leftover debris of childhood that no longer reflected who I was becoming.

Clearly at a crossroad, I was beginning to remember more deeply who I was on levels not yet fully realized. Those memories were essential to help me recognize and understand who I had become so that I could survive and grow in the environments of my childhood and adulthood. I had never fully questioned, or should I say challenged, the origins of my inner life of thoughts and feelings before that time.

It was easy to mistake my perceptions and beliefs for gospel, as if it were sacrilegious to question the validity of my own views and reactions. They seemed so inseparable from who I believed myself to be that, somehow, they became like sacred cows that were not to be disputed. Maybe it is the way I paid homage to the first sources of identity that befriended me in my initial efforts to find a place in the world. Even in moments of ecstatic opening, I found myself grieving the loss of these earlier times of shared experiences when we were first beginning to discover what it meant to be human.

I began to realize that to leave the "house" of my youth there was a good deal of housekeeping that was required before I could more fully be released from its powerful grip. It is easy to devalue previous structures of life as we open to new larger visions of what is possible. Sometimes I feel like a sifter of memories, searching for diamonds through the sands of time that flow though the portals of my life. I often feel driven to sift and sift until the precious gems expose themselves, revealing meanings about the nature of my experiences that have remained hidden in the recesses of my being. I was slow to realize that the battles that raged on within my heart often reflected a striving for deeper clarity. The inner turmoil would continue until I was able to achieve some modicum of understanding of what lay at the depth of my struggle. I gradually discovered that I would not be free from the grip of my inner labors until I was able to behold those gems, those insights, that were mine and mine alone to realize.

I have often found that the purest gems lie in the darkest places. Until I was brave enough to enter these unexplored edges of consciousness, however, I began to realize that I would not be able to discern what I most needed to see to discover the basis of who I am. I was on a mission to retrieve myself from a long hiatus, and I was discovering that there were important things that I had to understand to do so. I recognized that I must be willing to hold in question everything I thought, felt, and believed and to be willing to ask the questions: "Is this mine?" or (if not mine) "Whose is it?" and "Where did this come from?" More than any time in my life, I became aware of contrasting experiences that were, on one hand, open, joyous, loving, and peaceful, and on the other, represented long-known inner voices which were characterized by self-importance, criticism, judgment, and fear. My task was to discern what was real and to determine who I was separate from the debris and shadows of long internalized feelings and attitudes.

When we are young, we are so permeable; we have little choice but to allow what enters from others to shape who we are and how we view ourselves and the world. Early childhood dependencies certainly overpower any semblance of inner agency that might possibly exist to mitigate the potency of these dynamics. Consequently, I, like others, adopted ways of being that were not at all reflective of who I really was at my core. These formative experiences defined my ideas about myself until, as an adult, they were no longer applicable to who I was discovering myself to be. Even then, I continued to take as my own and perpetuate much of what I had received from others. The internal battle that intensified began to reflect a loss of appetite for those ways and elements of life that once attracted me.

Something within me was dying, and I found myself faced with difficult choices about where I stood within this large universe of possibilities.

Disoriented and lost, no prior models appeared appropriate to guide my way through the morass of feelings and perceptions that were surfacing from my past and present. I found myself caught between despondency for the losses of meaning that characterized the tasks of earlier life and anger at the weight of carrying, for so long, those feelings taken in from others that suffocated and strangled my heart. No longer willing to be a host for the now unwelcome internalized energies that initially organized my character, I attempted to simply purge or push them out as if they were poisons that I was trying to expunge from my system. I somehow believed that with enough willpower I could just excise or segregate these long-assimilated parts of my personality. My anger somehow felt life-giving as I toiled to separate the wheat from the chaff of those aspects of self no longer true to what was surfacing from within. With the pains of labor amplifying, the core of who I was, however, was not yet separated from the outer shell of the past sufficiently enough for me to have solid footing as I was releasing my old identifications.

What I did not understand at the time was that it was not my old conditioning that I was attempting to release but, rather, my identification with it. I also had to remember the wisdom of the "middle way" to remain balanced as I consciously shed the skin of my preliminary identity while simultaneously beginning to channel the very powerful numinous energies emerging from a source that had been unconscious most of my life. To open myself to this very subtle experience that was growing within me, and to be able to recognize its truth beyond anything of which I was aware, required the greatest height of courage and faith. If not for what had taken seed and was growing powerfully within me, I would have turned back to the security of familiar ways that appeared to provide shelter from life's ambiguities. I could not turn back, however, to a collapsing life structure that had already served its purpose and was no longer sufficient to hold the weight of the tasks I now was facing as I navigated midlife. The life-giving anger, the desire to find and stand my ground in this deepening experience of Self, provided the energy I needed to remain steadfast as I struggled to gain traction as this new way of being was forming.

I once heard a teaching that when faced with the task of ridding ourselves of the grip of those parts of ourselves that no longer reflect who we are, how do we get rid of them? The answer that was provided was, "You can't kill them; all you can do is educate them."[21] I was coming to terms with the realization that we can never abandon our lived experiences; they live within us forever. Yet, we seem to be in a continual process of re-negotiating the terms of our inner relationships and of our understanding of what they mean to us as we travel along the continuum of our lives. The question for me at that time was, "What did it mean to educate or update these old voices that cycled through my consciousness or to re-negotiate the terms of inner and outer relationships that no longer reflected who I was becoming and how I experienced myself?" I didn't know it then, but I was at the precipice of learning something that would forever change my experience of life and my role within it.

As in all development, I believe that there is a process of ripening that can't be rushed or opened prematurely, even though we often wish to push things along sooner than they are meant to evolve. I am referring to the *awareness of our capacity to choose,* our ability to act as *agents* on our own behalf in informing and guiding our thoughts, feelings, impulses, and the larger direction of our lives. It is no mistake that this aspect lied dormant while I was taking in all the guidance the world had to offer. Until I found

---

[21] Robert Bly quoting Marie-Louise Von Franz from her film *A Gathering of Men.* Moyers, B. (Producer), (1990). *A Gathering of Men* [Film]. Public Broadcasting Service.

myself on equal footing with other fallible human beings who were now in positions of authority, it never fully occurred to me that I could judge the validity of that which I was previously expected to swallow wholesale. Slowly, I dismantled the pedestal that once raised others beyond human size; I began the painful yet productive process of coming to terms with my own vulnerabilities and the illusions that prevented me from realizing the common struggles that all human beings face.

Somehow, it was this softening, this realization that we are all at different places along the same continuum of Self-discovery, that made it possible for me to soften toward myself and the normal inner struggles I had come to denigrate and demonize.

Of all the things that sparked the memories of how I got from there to here, it was undoubtedly parenthood that aided me most in shifting my perspective from that of a child to that of an adult. It was now I who had become the source of the voices that would live on within my children, providing grist for their mill in working their way to a deeper appreciation of life. Every generation would like to believe that they have improved on the one before. Like many, I did my human best to provide the moral and ethical guidance they needed to become effective members of the human community. Through them, I could see myself from a new perspective and was beginning to recognize that most adults attempt to do their best within their limited capacities in the moment for better or worse. Through a father's eyes, I was acutely in touch with a sense of my own shortcomings and the growing awareness that much of what I was passing on to my children had been given from parent to child since the beginning of humanity. It was this realization that allowed me, not as a child but as an adult, to begin to hold open to question all that I had taken in from others and adopted as my own.

I began viewing myself as an adult who was now able to choose and to set the tone and direction of my own life. I felt as though I had attained a "place at the table" in deciphering truth from lies, while updating old notions about myself and the world that did not pass the test of further examination. I was becoming aware that the gift of choice required a certain edge of self-trust and an inner spaciousness that made possible a continual process of discernment. To sift through and differentiate old, borrowed thoughts and feelings from those originating from a more authentic place within, I realized that I could never assume that I was arriving at some static place of awareness or awakening. Beginning my human venture riding in the back seat as my life was steered by others, I discovered that it was now I who was taking the wheel and plotting the course of my own journey.

Along with the exhilaration of my newfound creative powers also came the weight of the awareness that it was I who played the leading role in the direction of my own life. The seminal question of "Who am I?" became not so much a philosophical or theoretical one but, rather, a practical and experiential process of discovery. I asked myself, "Who is this person named Shemah who is able to feel myself an agent of choice within my own life? Where do I come from, and what is my purpose in this human experience that I have been so fortunate to be granted?" Even today, I ask these questions of my self, and the awareness that echoes back has continued to evolve as I have made my way through the many incarnations of my lifespan. Rather than through the expectation of an answer, it is the *contemplation of the question* that now brings me to a deeper contact of that for which I am searching.

At one time aspiring to arrive at some defined awareness, I was surprisingly pleased in my discovery that *we never seem to arrive anywhere other than clearing away the debris that obstructs our experience of what has always lived within us.* Until I opened to a fuller experience of Self, I did not have the psychological distance necessary to make visible those long-internalized feelings and beliefs that had resided within me for so long. As a fish in water, I was initially unable to distinguish myself from the pond that I had inhabited. *I was like a fish in water continually searching for the water.* The enlargement of awareness that came at midlife grew my capacity to see through the false beliefs that I once thought were mine to carry. I began to engage in the creative task of deciding what, if anything, I wished to hold in this basket of identity I referred to as my "self." My discerning capacities were growing, and I began to appreciate the enormous level of discipline that is required to remain focused and clear about who we are while immersed in the stresses, dangers, and complexities of life. I could now see the great chasm between the sober realities of adulthood and the naive expectations of youth. It was a challenge to begin to release myself from the inflated expectations of youth and also remain present to the gravity and depth of the tasks ahead.

What appeared on the surface to be a burst of clarity became a rather tumultuous time of discovering what happens when your perceptions about self and others begin shifting by this degree of magnitude. It was like an earthquake with powerful tectonic pressures splitting apart old ways of being which forced me to account for the ways in which I engaged myself and every relationship that had developed along the way. Commencing to challenge and discard no longer applicable ideas that circled my thoughts for a lifetime, I began consciously searching my memories for the original owners of the feelings and beliefs that I had held as my own. Either in person or within my heart, I set about returning them to their owners, one by one. Not only did this feel empowering, but the experience of releasing myself from the chains that had for so long bound my self-perceptions also brought a discovery of inner freedom that I had not known existed.

I use the term "inner freedom" here with great thoughtfulness in that I feel that it is our birthright for our inner energies to flow freely without obstruction. It is the outer expression of our freedom, however, that is much more complicated given the billions of other souls with whom we share our environment. *The free expression of our individual energies, particularly in ways that are life-giving and free of harm for the larger collective, has always been a great challenge for humanity.* These questions percolated intensely as I grew beyond the middle period of my life and began to slowly unlock an experience of inner freedom, an awareness, that was opening to the source of life that holds all of us. It was this level of inner connection that eventually enabled me to release myself and others from the imprisoning perception that they, for me, were the source of love and security on which I depended. This was pivotal in that I had for so long been unable to express myself fully for fear that I would lose the love that I so anxiously perceived as conditional. Recognizing that the love that I was seeking had always, *unconditionally*, resided within enabled me to give and receive love more generously, more abundantly, and with less concern for its loss. This was a great revelation as I began to awaken to the reality that I was not the ultimate source of love and security for others as well. To come to witness that each of us is an expression of this one Source was an indescribable relief and clarified the ways that I could best express my love and care for others. The untangling of distorted ideas about who I was also made possible an experience of inner contact that I never could have imagined. I was beginning to feel more fully myself and to remember who I was beyond a lifetime of borrowed thoughts, feelings, and perceptions that shaped my earlier experience of self and world.

As awareness continued to surface, so did my growing appreciation of the challenges we face as human beings. We are creatures so ruled by the hardwiring of our innate drives and reactions, responses to life that serve us well when we first began learning to engage the world of others. The initial gifts of this programming, unfortunately, cause us so much unnecessary suffering when it continues to dominate our ways of being as we progress into later life. I was beginning to perceive the subtle distinctions between the True Self and our well-conditioned identities and to recognize just how difficult it is to discern one from the other. As a youngster, I imbued adults with so much more wisdom than they could possibly have developed and naively believed the world to be so much more evolved than it actually was. To soberly witness the extent of our human frailties and to appreciate just how difficult it is to awaken and operate beyond the grip of our basic instincts and conditioning was like pulling the curtain open upon the Wizard of Oz only to reveal an ordinary person where there was once thought to be a great sorcerer. To behold the degree to which most of us remain dominated and attached to ways of being unchanged from the first periods of life came slowly and painfully to me.

To see this in humanity was also to see this in myself and to appreciate the depth of the task and the discipline involved in Self-discovery. Without connection to a larger awareness of Self, I began to appreciate just how difficult it is to grasp the degree to which we are shaped by our beliefs and reactions to life. Without Self-awareness, we cannot see and take ownership of the ways in which we create the reality in which we find our lives. Without wakefulness, we cannot free ourselves from the dominance of our primal survival instincts, making difficult the spaciousness required for us to be informed and guided by our higher intentions. The flooding of realizations about our emergent human state, about my emergent state, eventually brought me to a life-size appreciation of the magnitude of the challenges confronting all of us in our efforts to evolve as human beings. I had begun to recognize and appreciate even the small efforts others make to take seriously their responsibilities toward themselves and the world of others. Without attunement to the countless levels of being, I realized that we are vulnerable to being overtaken by the powerful influence of archetypal energies, our personal conditioning and hard-wired, primal impulses that lie just below our awareness.

Along with my growing tenderness for the difficult plight of humanity's challenges came a reverence for those who were willing to suffer in their struggle to achieve the clarity and discipline that they so valued. I once heard a saying that "Love of God is pure when joy and suffering inspire an equal degree of gratitude."[22] The hard-earned joy of finding my way to this new realm of Being helped me to appreciate just what that meant. As the memories of my journey began to crystallize, I found that I could more readily reflect on the process that brought me across the threshold to a greater appreciation of my life. It became a great gift to be available to assist others struggling to open to these awarenesses. It has also become clearer to me why older cultures have sustained rights of initiation; it is the way that the elders can offer wise guidance to those who would otherwise remain caught, struggling, between the shores of old and new modes of being. Witnessing those who first experience, or should I say remember, who they are is such an honor and certainly one of the greatest treasures of my lifetime. In turn, it has been the act of supporting others along the path that unexpectedly has opened the world even larger for me as I approached the next chapter of my life.

---

[22] Weil, S. (1952). *Gravity and Grace* (E. Crawford & M. Ruhr trans.). Routledge Classics.

WINTER

The time will come

when, with elation

you will greet yourself arriving

at your own door, in your own mirror

and each will smile at the other's welcome

— Derick Walcot

Shemah (1987)

My fingertips were losing feeling. It had been 29 years since the warehouse trauma left me with the challenge of coping with an incurable, lifelong injury. The numbing was the first sign that my cervical discs had degenerated to a serious level. Daily headaches followed as my energies languished and movement became increasingly constricted, the pain consuming my thoughts and activities.

One evening, anxious about the progression of my symptoms, I found the courage to ask myself: "Have I learned everything from this injury that it was here to teach me?" I was pleasantly surprised as "Yes" echoed in my mind and heart and reverberated down my limbs. Receiving the green light of sorts, I searched for something to help mitigate my symptoms and provide some relief. I discovered a newly approved surgery that had, miraculously, just been made available. I was in the operating room within a month and on to recovery soon afterward.

A coincidence? At this point, I knew better. The injury had guided me onto a path I, otherwise, would have missed entirely. It was my albatross and my guru, creating suffering I could not shake; yet, that suffering definitely shook away the dross that blinded me from my True Being. After those very long years of completing the lesson, the surgery successfully released me from a lifetime of pain and opened the door to "freedom." Freedom from physical pain was just the beginning of my emancipation from the prison bars of identity that incarcerated me from my true Self. That light within, no longer "separate" from me, was flowing into memory, modifying, and sensitizing cells to receive a form of being long dormant to consciousness. After years of disassembling, I was finally becoming reassembled in a shape that matched my soul.

One morning, post-surgery, the aroma of freshly brewed Italian roast coffee wound its way through the house, alerting me that my wife was in the kitchen preparing our usual poached eggs and wheat toast. In the bathroom mirror, looking at my 65-year-old visage, I startled as I began to shave, seeing the image of my old friend who had entered my life when I was 8 years old, dear Cornelius. My hair, now white like his, and a countenance reflecting the bitter sweetness of life's journey, superimposed onto his like a double image coming into focus, blending into one.

Eventually, I had to blink. It was just me in the mirror, but that "me" also was Cornelius in my heart of hearts and had been all along. It was as if waking up from a dream with the knowledge that you had been dreaming, your mind's eye seeing the beautiful orchestration that leads us away from ourselves and then back again. I finished shaving and walked to the kitchen to kiss my wife: "Good morning, dear. Breakfast looks beautiful, and the coffee *smells so good. Have I told you how much I love you lately?" She smiled, and we drank our brew while reading the morning news.*

"Why did it take me so long to come to this place?" I mused. So many times, I seemed to come to an ending only to realize I was just beginning, twisting, and turning, retracing my steps, trying to shortcut but getting stuck in the hedges. Only now do I see, with the calling received when I was 35 just beginning to manifest, and the path clear ahead: regardless of how old the soul, I couldn't have skipped any of the stages, no matter how precocious. Rounding the last corner toward the exit, the privilege and preciousness of elderhood comes into full view as the labyrinth of life is entirely revealed. Returning to full consciousness, I remember: everything I do and have done flows, and has always flowed, into the larger family of souls.

Winter // Author

The two contrasting streams that, on one hand, gradually reveal the unfolding structure of being and, on the other, provide intimate, lived experience of the process of self-discovery slowly converge as the disparate sides of our experience of life seek to become one. This draw of consciousness toward a unity of perspective and identity seems to allow us to release ourselves from the dominance of earlier ways of being. It also appears to open us to our full creative potential and a desire to give back. There is a Sufi saying that the first stage of life is like "making honey," the second involves "tasting honey," the third "becoming honey," and the last, "serving honey." As the story continued, I felt as if I was being served the honey that had become sweetened over a lifetime. Nonetheless, I could feel Shemah slipping away more and more with each meeting, repositioning himself ever closer to what lies beyond as the last veil that separates this side from the other began to fall. I found myself feeling both grateful and sad as his eyes slowly dimmed, yet I was eager to engage the last leg of his journey.

Winter // Cornelius

The soul is like a luminous stone with an infinite number of facets. Life circumstances we choose, the platforms we create through the seasons of life, and the experiences that attract us all shape the direction in which our lives evolve. Specific qualities, that become the dominant focus of our development, represent a small sample of the entirety of Being and the infinite possibilities that were ours from which to choose before entering this medium. While in the human state, it is a fallacy to believe that some aspects are more useful or important than others or that we will ever complete the evolution of those facets of consciousness that we enter to refine. As the end of our time approaches, it is difficult to appreciate that our purpose is not to bring our expansion to a conclusion but, rather, to find meaning in the life that is ours to create during our precious journey.

We can never judge nor take stock of any other life, as our joy and desire lie not in comparison with other souls but in the endless possibilities of refinement and clarity of each unique aspect of our being, and ours alone. The waters and sands of life wash against each soul in unique ways, sculpting, polishing, and maturing qualities that emerge as we live within and through our life experiences. These living images that we carry with us through the seasons of life are like no others and can only be fully appreciated by the one in whom they arise. Valuing our own unique trajectory and the decisions that shape the character of our life also makes possible a deeper acceptance of the paths not taken and choices not made regarding the dimensions of the soul that have yet to be refined. As we develop into greater awareness of our limitless possibilities, we are not only able to better embrace the fruits of our own incomplete journeys but also are able to better witness the unique beauty and gifts of others as they engage their own distinct, chosen paths.

Within the context of new possibilities of emerging consciousness during the winter period of life lies also the increasingly concrete reality of our finitude. This awareness provides the impetus to begin to prepare for the end of our human journey. Increasing pressures caused by these dual and often competing realities spur us to begin to create the fourth and last platform of life. The crafting of the fourth platform involves the very challenging process of locating a new position that will enable us to achieve both an enduring openness and also intentful preparation for the conclusion of our voyage through the seasons.

The energy that calls us home to our original state is the same energy that draws us to engage more deeply in our lives. Presence and transcendence are ultimately two sides of the same position. We transcend through presence, not through escape or dissociation. ***There is no bypass or shortcut to awakening.*** Our shifting life structure as we become older, more experienced pilgrims is accompanied by an ever-increasing pull from our inner presence. Experiences of these gathering energies are affected significantly by what remains of identification with our conditioning as we move through the summer and fall periods of life. Capacities to create the platforms needed to foster development within each life period make possible gradual conscious re-alignment with our center of being. A more integrated relationship with the larger Self also holds the possibility of greater connection with our depths and creative freedom that enables us to form intentions unencumbered by the limiting perspectives of our early conditioning.

From a wider lens, we must remember that each soul's evolution is unique and that the parameters of a chosen incarnation will impact one's capacity for an individuated life in different ways. We should not assume that all individuals will or should be able to endure the labors of death and rebirth necessary to expand beyond the identification with the ego-self, nor should we presume that each life comes with the intention or circumstances necessary to do so. The hero's journey for one life might be to seek awareness born from a deep immersion within the inescapable complexities, dangers, and challenges of a difficult existence (e.g., severe disability, famine, or war), while another soul might pursue the very demanding and subtle discipline of conscious evolution transcendent of the limitations of mere human survival and conditioning. For those who do choose the path of individuated consciousness, however, crossing the critical nexus at midlife is often a disorienting and agonizing process as it enlarges our scope of awareness and leads us to the possibility of a re-centering of consciousness and identity. While not all individuals are able to successfully make this journey, the metamorphosis of the middle passage holds the possibility of a profound re-alignment with a larger, more authentic ground of Self. Those who establish this new centering of personality, who *choose* to subordinate the ego-self to the larger Being from which it arose (Self), are able to discover a living balance between the spaciousness of the transcendent and the constriction of the immanent, offering a potential experience of an undivided state as the psyche evolves a harmonious relationship between the conditioned and unconditioned poles of being.

While the ongoing emergence of consciousness is clearly at the heart of the human journey, the completion of certain conditions is, first, necessary for us to successfully and fully unfold as the process of life continues. If we are to fulfill our potential for wholeness, the platforms that enable us to achieve expanding awareness must become sufficiently consolidated as developmental milestones are reached. The foundations that hold us as we travel through each season of life, however, are fragile and highly susceptible to rupture by events that arrest the healthy maturation of the heart (e.g., physical and/or emotional trauma, addiction, mental illness), causing our deeper emotional being to become disconnected and inaccessible to our conscious life. Early emotional fractures that *dis-member* us from parts of our inner reality ultimately weaken the structure and cohesiveness of the developing ego-identity and can leave it vulnerable and unable to endure inevitable encounters with the emerging Self without fragmentation or regression (see image below). Emotional dissociation, most importantly, can leave the Self isolated without the partnership with ego that is necessary for continued differentiation, maturation, and eventual embodiment as it strives to become the center of psychic life. Lastly, the absence of initiations and cultural traditions designed to facilitate developmental transitions from one life period to another leaves us with a tendency to remain captive within earlier constructions of self-identification.

Healthy and Unhealthy Ego-Self Relationship

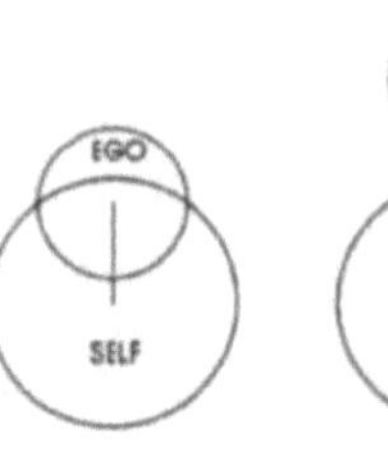
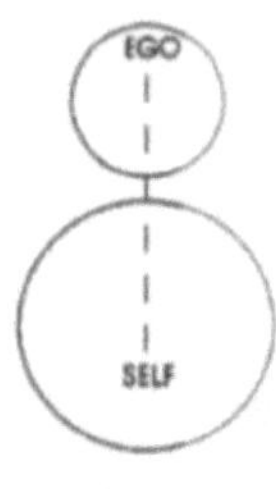
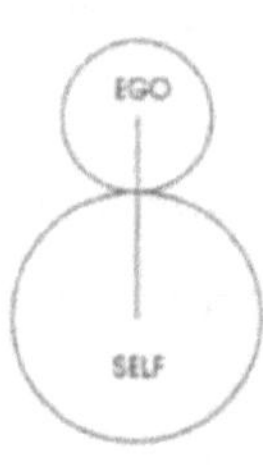
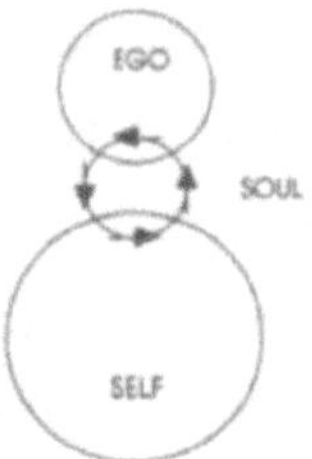

PSYCHOSIS (Ego-Self axis unconscious)   **DEPRESSION ALIENATION** (Ego-Self axis ruptured)   **HEALTHY** (Ego-Self axis conscious)   **INDIVIDUATION** (Ego-Self loop animating)

MADNESS, RELIGIOUS EXPERIENCE, AND THE WISDOM TO KNOW THE DIFFERENCE
February 3, 2021
with Thomas Patrick Lavin, PhD,, Jung institute of Chicago

We naturally resist birthing into new consciousness and, therefore, benefit greatly from being guided and midwifed so we may learn to relax into and align with our continuing expansion. As our hearts mature, we are better able to consciously remain open to the polarities (good/evil) that are so difficult to reconcile and presence when we are younger. We also may discover that an open, compassionate heart makes possible an inner position that is receptive to reclaiming and re-membering *all* shadow elements that have become split off, disowned, and disregarded. *Nonetheless, we must be clear that it is necessary for our hearts to be connected with the eternal source of life for it to have the capacity to remain present to all that passes through it; the human heart, alone, is incapable of presencing the fullest depth of experience and feeling without direct, conscious relationship with the infinite ocean of Being.* After a lifetime of building upon and "leaving" earlier developmental platforms (i.e., 1) undifferentiated Oneness, 2) parental / family ground, and 3) conditioned / preliminary self), it may feel counterintuitive to reorient and "return" to the original foundations of who we are. This "*turn of step*," however, is a necessary rapprochement for us to engage the possibility of a new experience of Unity which is now conscious and highly integrated.

We spend the first half of our lives engaged in the heroic task of leaving the original ground of being, of enduring multiple levels of differentiation from world, from body, from mind, from spirit, as we struggle to create a functional platform of self that can withstand the very challenging and mysterious return to wholeness. This next, and last leg, of the "Hero's Journey" is once, again, a path through many layers. But this passage is not of leaving but of engaging the most difficult task of returning to and embracing the full dimensions of who we are, of re-integration to a conscious unification of spirit, mind, body, and world (see image below). Moreover, our *return* to Self is also characterized by a continuous call to a sacred wedding, a harmonization of fully matured masculine and feminine energies, to the unification of the transcendent and immanent dimensions of Being, to embracing both the good and evil that live within all of us, and to welcoming the love and wisdom that is the foundation of who we are. This process holds the potential of culminating in a new level of integration as the Self becomes embodied and the material dimension becomes *ensouled.* The alchemists refer to this most integrated level of being as the "philosopher's stone." This journey also represents a return to our matriarchal foundations. What began with leaving the mother now involves a return, not to mother but to *Sophia* (the goddess of knowledge and wisdom), the Ground of Being, in which matter and spirit are consciously unified to achieve the highest state of spiritual development.[23]

---

[23] Neumann, E. (1949). *The Origins and History of Consciousness,* originally published in German as *Ursprungsgeschichte des Bewusstseins* by Rascher Verlag, Zürich.

THREE STAGES OF DIFFERENTIATION AND RE-INTEGRATION

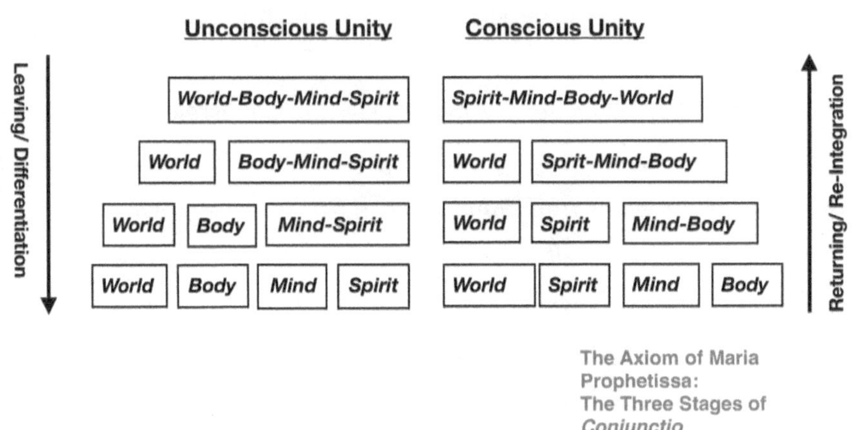

The Axiom of Maria Prophetissa:
The Three Stages of *Coniunctio*
August J. Cwik, Psy.D.
Jung Institute of Los Angeles, 2021

Reliance on coping patterns that resist our call to wholeness will not mitigate the powerful pull of the emerging Self during the winter period, however. Remnants of our attachments to the preliminary self will cause us to continue to operate within a duality of consciousness. The perception or experience that Life Force energy remains outside of our self-regulation might also persist. The degree to which our experience continues to be that these phenomena originate from an external source powerfully influences the direction and form our lives may take in their closing chapters. *It is often our deepest good or greatest evil that remains projected outside of our personal identity so that we can attempt to maintain a simple inner integrity.* If we are unable to expand to lovingly embrace all aspects of S/self, we will continue to be divided within and threatened by the emergence of natural, growing awareness. The leaves that drop during fall and winter are the precious memories borne from a lifetime immersed in human experience. This falling away offers us the psychological distance necessary to sift through and gather those memories that bring our lives into a broader perspective. Consequently, some of us may come to realize the responsible role we play in creating our own reality, while others may continue to experience their realities as determined by powers external to the self and beyond their personal influence.

As we age, continued lack of awareness of the nature by which our thoughts and feelings regulate the flow of subtle energies contributes to the likelihood of added physical decline, particularly as our bodies grow less able to tolerate the restriction of this energy supply. An enduring belief that the Source of Life lies beyond our purview of conscious relationship tends to leave us feeling fearful and powerless; habitual clinging to identifications of earlier periods of life significantly impedes our ability to pursue the higher creativity and freedom that is possible in the latter years. The inability to be re-born into greater consciousness of our origins during midlife also makes it difficult, if not impossible, for us to provide the sustenance and guidance that the youth so greatly need as they navigate the treacherous waters of their own journeys.

The ability to negotiate a profound reorganization of our conscious center of Self during midlife creates the foundation for the direction that our paths may take during the second half of life. A multitude of possible life directions appear as we begin to move further into the winter period, ones that often segregate older pilgrims into dramatically different modes as they orient themselves toward their final years. *In this latter period of life, there are "elders" and there are "olders."* In varying degrees, individuals tend to move either toward solidifying their attachments to those concerns of the pre-midlife self or in the direction of *remembering who they are.* The emergence of Essential energy continues to intensify in elderhood as the powers of the body wane and the light of the authentic Self more fully waxes. Clutching to earlier modes of identity may become much like clinging to a sinking ship as the end of life approaches. It also becomes increasingly apparent that we cannot fully engage the larger cycle of life as midwives to others unless we, ourselves, have had the blessing of crossing the threshold into fuller awareness.

As the responsibilities of parenthood and work lighten, the counterbalance of diminishing physical energies reminds us of the preciousness of our remaining time. Awareness of the value of time leads us to more attentively prioritize how we might wish to engage the involvements of our closing years. After a lifetime of weighty commitments, we often take the route of using our newfound freedom to detach from the concerns and struggles of those within earlier seasons of life. This can unfortunately lead to increased self-absorption, isolation, and a loss of purpose at a time when we have the greatest potential for creative generativity and the transmission of the fruits of our hard-earned wisdom. Never having experienced the grief and celebration that accompany life's principal transitions, we may be unable or unwilling to open ourselves to the new possibilities of elderhood. We might, instead, remain encumbered by life's regrets and our struggle to cope with the dissolution of the body and the self to which we may have become so firmly identified.

The cycle of life cannot fully turn without the necessary contributions of those within each seasonal phase. As we settle further into the winter period, we may begin to discover the ways in which human interdependencies call upon each generation to mutually assist and initiate one another though the critical thresholds of life. Like an infant's cry causing mother's milk to flow abundantly from the breasts, the calls of youth also induce the elder to offer the food of love and wisdom to those in need of its sustenance. In turn, through the act of giving, the conscious opening to this calling provides meaning and purpose to later life and initiates us further into the mysteries of the next transitional experience of physical death and return to our original state.

The winter period of life offers profound opportunities for those able to align courageously and consciously with the gravitational pull of Self as it intensifies. The evolving presence of Authentic Being is a dynamic and emergent process in the winter phase. Engagement with the progressive expansion of our relationship with the Self requires opening channels that regulate the flow of the life force within our bodies. An act of conscious surrender is necessary to allow ourselves to stretch to new levels of receptivity as the influx of energy flows into awareness. Each increment of enlarging consciousness is likely, however, to inflame those wounded areas of the heart that continue to resist opening to the loving and joyous energy that emanates from the center of being. We must be brave when presencing those delicate places of the soul that have been injured by the harsher edges of life. Willingness to explore these areas of suffering may allow us to bring new, compassionate attention to old traumas, to honor our grief for life's losses, and to begin to release long-held attachments that separate us from our True Nature.

Loss of friends and loved ones, as well as our youthful appearance, vigor, and cognitive fluidity all come with the territory of winter. Releasing from these powerfully held attachments of identity can be a source of great sadness as we crystallize awareness of the events and circumstances that have characterized our journey through the seasons. While quite painful and, at first, disorienting, the death of identification with the preliminary self makes possible the lifting of the veil that maintains the illusion of separation from Source of Being. Seeking to reconcile with the past and negotiate the certainty of physical death, we may find ourselves at a crossroad in which repetitive attempts to complete the garment of life potentially gives way to emerging presence. The quickening death of identification with the "provisional"[3] self miraculously opens us to a vastness in which we may begin to glimpse more fully the wondrous mystery from which all life originates.

Building upon the earlier platforms of spring, summer, and fall, the intentful cultivation of the fourth platform offers an extension or bridge into the realm of Greater Being, giving us a foothold that allows us to stand more firmly in both the physical and non-physical dimensions. Securely rooted from a lifetime planted within the soil of human life, newfound abilities to see through the eyes of the Unconditioned Self allow us to witness that everything is alive with Energy. We may then discover that there is only one true place to stand, and that is in the *eternal now*. As resistance to the interminable flame of life diminishes, so will the experience of separation that creates the perception of duality between self and other. The realization of life's oneness represents the final pieces in the process of conscious re-membering. *Re-membering is both the realization of the truth of our origins as well as an intentful process of re-constructing the seemingly unrelated pieces of our lives so we may begin to see the whole of our creative expansion.*

Gratitude that flows from those who achieve a broader perspective in elderhood reflects an appreciation, as well as the hard-earned awareness, of the meaning of both the joy and suffering that is inherent in human experience. The ability to begin to see more of the whole of life also makes possible the release of long-felt anger and disappointment toward those people and events that were once perceived as the source of our suffering. Gradual distance from conditioned patterns of thinking and feeling also allow us to more objectively observe the nature of when, where, and how these repetitive tapes became rooted within the voices of our consciousness. Until we become aligned with the felt resonance of our True Nature and can observe our thoughts and feelings with some level of detachment, we cannot begin to direct our life energies in a more intentional manner.

The fourth platform of winter makes possible a new, reorganized relationship to life energy within the body. The integrity of elderhood holds the potential of a consciously directed flow of creative intentionality within the world, reflecting a connection and commitment not only to our unique being but also to the universe as a whole. Few develop awareness of the unity that underlies our experiences. Gratitude for those people who were able and willing to light the way for those of us in need of example and guidance comes as we begin to appreciate the significance of the gift that was given. The cycle of the seasons is like an interwoven fabric that leads simultaneously away from itself and also back upon itself, revealing that if any thread goes missing, the fabric falls to pieces. The same is so with the relationship to those within and between the seasons of human life.

Programmed into the unfolding of the human organism are original instructions or archaic images that exist to provide a guiding map for our development. These images, or archetypes, give form to the seasonal tasks and platforms that aid us as we negotiate the demands of each life period. The image of the *"Elder"* is alive in the consciousness of each individual as we move through the winter period, partly as memory from our youth, partly as archetypal programming, partly as social construction, and partly as the lived experience of one who has developed into a position of maturity and awareness. Allowing our elderhood to become shaped exclusively by memories, social expectations, and archetypal images can become overly confining when we align ourselves with an identity that is not consistent with our authentic unfolding. This can represent another form of attachment at a time when the possibility of opening to joy and freedom is at its height.

Instruction or direction will not help younger pilgrims to connect the threads of the seasons; true wisdom is the disciplined act of guidance by example. We cannot teach love, joy, or harmony; we can only *be* love, joy and harmony. To become a living embodiment of maturity is the greatest of gifts to those younger pilgrims struggling blindly in the darkness when the Essence is naturally dormant. When we see others in periods of difficulty, it is natural for us to compassionately attend to their suffering by joining with their pain. *We cannot, however, assist others by uniting with their suffering. We can lead them to clarity only by remaining firmly aligned with the peace that is our True Selves.* The light of Authentic Being must remain lit to guide others through the stormy nights of the soul. Allowing ourselves to relax into this knowledge is one of the gifts and fruits of elderhood. Yet, without the hunger and calling of younger pilgrims in need of the "food" that elders can provide, the inspiration to maintain this awareness can easily become lost. Humble acknowledgement of the important gifts that each offers one another ultimately bonds the generations together in loving appreciation.

Humility is a position of being no more and no less than we are. Releasing ourselves from inflated images or lowered expectations of how life should be lived frees us to live more openly and honestly in the authentic moment. This also makes possible the opportunity to experience the love that is natural when beings allow connection with one another without fear or expectation. The ability to consciously remain open in the face of old, habitual reactions that once restricted the flow of energy makes possible a new experience of inner freedom. This experience of conscious Self-regulation allows us to remain in a loving, open-hearted position less dominated by the once overshadowing influences of inner or outer conditions. It also consistently makes available the experience of love that is the truth of our nature and origins. From this position, we may truly be able to harness our full creative energies simply from the basis of remembering who we are. Ultimately, those creations arising from the center of being are the gifts we would like to leave to this wondrous place that has been so instrumental in our expanded awareness.

Preparation for transition presents us with our final leap of faith into a gap-space in which we are no longer tethered to the material body, brain, and ego-self. As with many passages before, we are, again, faced with releasing from a known structure into a larger experience of Self, the original state of being. This, we call the *Third and last Death–Re-Birth within the human life cycle*. Each seasonal platform offers us further depth and subtlety; continued opening toward our boundless nature calls for the renewal of faith and a willingness to surrender ways of being that have once been meaningful and sustaining. It is our ceaseless curiosity for the mystery of our journey that ultimately draws us (through birth, death, and rebirth) to release into subtler and subtler expressions of spirit.

As we enter our final hours, we might continue to question the meaning of our journey and the significance of our presence to those who will follow us. From within the confines of individual consciousness, however, it is difficult to fathom that each of us is but one *small* facet of an infinitely articulated diamond. Each fraction of light, from each individual point of reference, released in expanded awareness contributes to the overall brightness and clarity of light of larger Being. As we evolve, we may each contribute without full awareness of how we affect one another and the whole of creation. We will know it in the faces of our loved ones in our parting moments and in the joy and appreciation that fills our hearts as we are received again in the loving arms of our origins. When we are home again, we remember the intensity of the forces that generate new consciousness where only ideas once existed. Walking through the fires of human life shines a mirror to the soul that allows us to see and know ourselves more clearly. The bitterness and the sweetness of this clarity is what brings us into greater connection with ourselves and into greater unity with all Being as it ever-expands.

It is these well-earned gifts of the venture through the vicissitudes of human life that bring us to return to the deep well of creation and drink over and over again.

Winter // Shemah

As I began my transition into old age, I experienced a craving to begin to concentrate my energies on dreams and desires that had remained elusive during most of my earlier adulthood. I was feeling a strong pull to turn to my inner life as I was gradually letting go of outer demands of long-held responsibilities. Serendipitously, I happened upon a poem at that time that resonated deeply for me. It went something like this: "Throw yourself like a seed as you walk, and into your own field; don't turn your face for that would be to turn it to death, and do not let the past weigh down your motion...from your work you will one day be able to gather yourself."[24] Interestingly, a vision of the tasks-at-hand seems to reveal itself when the time appears ripe for understanding. The time was ripe, and I had begun the process of reclaiming or harvesting what had been growing within me over a lifetime.

I had clearly given the greater part of my life to casting my seeds into the fields of others, often neglecting what seemed to be mine to attend to as I moved forward. I hold no regrets for where I placed my energies; the tasks of early survival and apprenticeship required that I learn to work the fields that others had created so that one day I might be able to plant and tend to my own garden with greater skill and mastery. The fruits of my

---

[24] Unamuno, M. (1992). "Throw Yourself Like Seed". In R. Bly, J. Hillman & M. Meade (Eds.), *The Rag and Bone Shop of the Heart: A Poetry Anthology* (p. 234). HarperCollins Publishers.

planting, whether in my own fields or those of others, have come back to me tenfold. I began to understand that planting and tending to my own garden would make it possible for me to give of myself in ways that were new and even more abundant.

By this time in my life, I had been married for many years, and my children had begun to build lives and families of their own. I was emancipating from a long tour of duty of working for others and placing my own dreams in the background of life's priorities. I felt as if I was leaving a level of reality that was both loved and encumbering, and definitely one that encouraged a tendency to commit my energies in ways that were not always consistent with my soul's longing. The pull that drew my energies outward, however, began to conflict with deeper stirrings that were calling me to attend to something that was coalescing on levels not yet articulated. I was becoming an old man, or older anyway. I had not yet come to terms with what this meant as my life was moving beyond parenthood and the stresses and obligations that many younger adults take for granted while they are immersed in the busyness of life. My time was being freed up at the same moment that I was realizing that I had much less of it left to live.

It was certainly a challenge for me to reconcile that my sense of my life was feeling fuller at a time when I also was feeling the emptiness and grief of times gone by and the regrets of missed opportunities. I was feeling the beginnings of leaving and was preparing to engage in the contemplation of what it meant to be approaching the end of my time here on earth. A dear friend of mine, who referred to himself as a "Basketarian,"[25] would often remind me of all the things we carry in our baskets of identity, e.g., internalized feelings, thoughts, anxieties, and conflicts that are *not ours to shoulder*, weighing us down and preventing us from experiencing a fuller sense of our True Selves. This was a time of taking inventory of what was

---

[25] Leonard M. Zunin, M.D.

in my basket and beginning to let go of the things that were no longer relevant to the next steps of my journey. We unknowingly hold onto so many elements of life and relationship that we take into our field of self, and yet, for me, some were filled with memories so dear that I wept for days as I released myself of their enduring grip. I also found myself asking for and offering forgiveness for all those mutual infractions and injuries that accumulate along the way as we struggle to share our lives with one another.

Where once it had been love, money, acquiring knowledge, and other things of perceived worth, it was now *time* and the *vitality* to use it well that had become the valued commodities that organized my priorities. I was acutely aware of my dwindling energies and the limited time I had left to express them. Taking stock of my precious moments, I realized how often I attempted to cultivate gardens in soil that was void of the nutrients and waters of life necessary to promote their growth. I often learned the hard way(s) that I was giving energy to projects and persons where no mutuality existed and where the very remote potential for something to blossom was obvious to everyone but me. Growing perspective, however, was allowing me to divine better where the soils were fertile, and life flowed with greater abundance.

To a Renaissance man, or even to one who scatters his energies about in all directions, coming to terms with the idea that the best of worlds lied in my own backyard required the capacity to let go of many life-long attachments. I was finding it much less difficult to let go of earlier identifications that held and clothed me so that I could one day "gather" myself. This falling away of layers of previous incarnations made possible the recognition of the beauty of the subtleties not yet appreciated by those still in youth. I was becoming one of those subtleties, feeling myself somewhat invisible to those of the younger generation. It's amazing how so much becomes visible in the realm of old age, only to discover that what has taken a lifetime to incubate is neither perceptible nor valued by those who are still in the formative years of their lives.

What was once invisible and too subtle to perceive was now becoming palpable and surprisingly obvious. This clarity of aging made possible the apprehension of larger patterns that are embedded within a text that is only apparent with awareness of the sacred. When I became present enough to begin to perceive the subtle intertwining threads underlying the mysterious web of life, I found that I could somehow identify a distinct path where before there had been many possibilities. To see *my* doorway among the many options simplified my priorities in ways that allowed me to concentrate my energies in more life-giving and fertile directions. I was no longer willing to cast my pearls in ways that were not consonant with the refinement of my priorities and found myself becoming increasingly able to discern the ways and with whom I chose to spend my precious, remaining moments. While I realize that these moments have always been precious, never before had I understood just how precious each was.

I began to see now why older people become "short" with others and not reluctant to express their irritations openly when faced with inconsequential situations. The limitations of time and the unwillingness to waste precious energies can make us very demanding and irritable about just how, where, and with whom we want to spend our dwindling capital. I was certainly no different and was becoming clearer about what was important to me and how I wished to use the precious time left within this slowly declining body. I found myself surrounded by others of my generation struggling with the stresses of aging, fearing the loss of youthful appearance, health, and an honored place within society. I was experiencing a definite crossing over into old age, but this was of a different quality from that which I had experienced during other life transitions. It was unclear just what this crossing entailed and what was required of me to find a sense of worth when faced with the threat of invisibility, isolation, and obsolescence.

I once heard a saying that when making the passage into deeper territories of the Self, we must "pay the boatman." I would ask myself: "What did this mean for me at this juncture of life? What currency did I possess to offer for this crossing, and what was this mysterious place across the river to which the boatman would transport me?" I had been releasing a great deal in this period of time, some by my own volition and so much, reluctantly, with grief of the profound losses that naturally come with age. I had lost so many of my loved ones; my hair had grown gray and thinning, and my face formed new wrinkles daily as earth's gravity pulled my body ever closer to the soil from which I sprouted.

I had enjoyed the healthy glow and youthful attractiveness of my early adulthood. I created a bountiful career and a beautiful marriage and family with a community of very dear friends. Looking in the mirror, I eventually began to see someone I could no longer recognize. And, yet, in my heart, I was sensing someone whom I had known for a very long time. It was as if an old friend were emerging from somewhere deep within me, someone who had long ago stepped into the shadows of my life so that I could find my way into this world. It was wonderful to sense and welcome him once again.

With so many around me clinging to old images no longer reflected in the physical mirror, I found myself striving to look beyond burdensome societal definitions of beauty, vigor, and financial worth. The weight of values that once felt like worthy challenges toward which to aspire began to feel like heavy baggage that I was no longer willing or able to carry. I was realizing that the boatman would not accept any baggage, not even a carry-on. To make the crossing, I would have to bring only that which was essential, and that would be limited to my True Self whom I was, again, befriending. The price the boatman was asking was, indeed, a steep one, and one many of my generation were unwilling to pay. What initially felt like a great sacrifice was, in fact, my salvation and the greatest gift of my life.

I had always heard that old people spend much time in review of their lives, but I didn't understand exactly what this was about until I arrived, engaged in my own process of reflection; I found myself deeply involved in the cycling and recycling of memories and feelings I thought had long ago been laid to rest. What was the purpose of sorting through old memories and circumambulating them as if in search of a unique angle or new doorway into old, crystallized images? I remembered a loved poem that ended with "it is not unusual to sift through ashes and find an *unburnt* picture."[26] I was, indeed, sifting through ashes but was not completely sure what I would discover as I circled closer to the still-burning embers of unfelt, or should I say unlived, experiences. I found myself stumbling upon old memories, unexpectedly experiencing them like forgotten friends that I had cast out into the cold long ago. In my youth, I did not have the courage or the understanding to welcome them into my newly forming house of self.

I felt like the king in the story of the prodigal son that was now welcoming home all evicted or abandoned pieces of my experience, re-collecting those split-off shards of Self without which I would not have been able to discover the picture which was left "unburnt." I was learning to forgive myself for my many mistakes, transgressions, and unrealistic expectations that caused me to turn away from myself in shame and self-loathing. Finding acceptance, and even a sense of love and appreciation

---

[26] Giovanni, N. (1975). "The Women Gather". In *The Women and the Men: Poems*. Morrow.

of all the understandable foibles that make us human, enabled me to experience something unexpectedly whole and untarnished at my core.

Searching the corners of my past, I was metabolizing aspects of experience apparently too painful or difficult to have been embraced in my younger years. "What had changed that was allowing me to hold within the scope of my heart what had been beyond my capacities even during the challenging fires of midlife?" I asked myself. I was experiencing a gradual burning away of the debris that had separated me from who I was discovering myself to be. Something large, expanding, and very old was enabling me to remain compassionately present to that which previously would have been quite fragmenting or overwhelming. A memory of my Self was opening like a flower, evaporating old fears and reassuring me that I would not fall into an abyss. I felt as if I were coming home after a long journey, finally arriving to fully bear witness to the life I had been living, or not living, for many years.

Clearly, I was gathering myself and harvesting what had laid unconscious and dormant for most of my life. I was feeling a sense of abundance that only comes when you know that what flows within you comes from an unlimited source. The fullness that flowed from my center lay in stark contrast to the scarcity that had so long characterized my sense of the availability and conditionality of life energies. My experience of Self was no longer feeling personal but, rather, like a reflection of something endless, limitless, and interconnected. To feel my Self reaching beyond personal borders began to give clues to the unity that I saw existing within even contrasting and disparate forms. A lifetime of withholding and self-protection was giving way to a clearer sensibility of just how much we all need to feel connected and loved, and just how difficult this simple truth is for us to enact while we walk the labyrinth of our lives.

What had called me inward to gather lost or abandoned pieces of myself was now turning outward; *when the eternal waters of life flow abundantly through us, they cannot be contained or withheld within and only for oneself.* The distinction between giving and receiving mysteriously began to melt away. I found myself called to give my attention and energy to a world that, I realized, needed those who were ready and able to provide the food harvested from the breadbasket of a long life. This was no doubt a time of rebirth for me into a form of being that I have so come to cherish. I had no interest in segregating myself as some older people often do or elevating myself above others as if I were one who had attained some height of wisdom. I felt that there is a purpose in living long enough to achieve a certain embodiment of Self-awareness, and I wished to offer myself in service and take my place among those ready to give back, in gratitude, for the gift of life.

I have often heard the saying, "Youth is wasted on the young." I have come to believe that this saying was derived from those who had not discovered the blessings and meaning of old age. I feel just the opposite; *old age is often wasted on the old,* given that some are inclined to back away from the sacred tasks of aging or withhold the unique gifts that are theirs alone to bestow upon the young. It was not easy to know how to return to the world, however, when it is not clear that the youth want what I most had to give at this time of my life. We somehow expect the young to be able to see and appreciate those invisible qualities that have taken us so many years to gestate. It is not their job to value us, I believe; it is for us to know the values of which they are in the greatest need so we can offer what is of most use to them in successfully navigating the very challenging obstacles of their lives. If we have not come to this place within ourselves and are still identified with the conditioning in which they remain captive, then we may have very little to offer them. If we haven't evolved a larger experience of who we are, we are more likely to burden them with our unresolved struggles than to be someone who can guide them through difficult times.

I feel endlessly fortunate to have lived long enough to see a number of generations bud and blossom before my eyes. I never imagined the joys involved in nurturing the hearts of children again as I had experienced while developing into grandparenthood. It was as if we were meeting at two ends of the cycle of life, one not yet having lost the purity and innocence of the Self with which he entered, and I re-discovering a long-lost friend after a lengthy process of reclaiming what had become dormant many years before. No longer having the primary responsibility for teaching them the ropes of adapting, I found myself free to align simply with the tender beauty of their hearts and the desires of their souls and to give what had taken me a lifetime to cultivate. I discovered, however, that it was they who had the most to give to me, somehow possessing the key to levels of myself that could not have been opened simply through the process of recollection. It was they who connected me with the beauty and joy of my beginnings that were untarnished by the transfigurations of life's immense challenges.

Giving to young souls also helped me further to find a new position that was forming in ways that were very different from the evolving foundations of my younger days. As a young man, I felt that I had to prove myself to feel entitled to holding a place of value in the world. I felt that I had to "go to battle" to assert or defend the precious ground that I believed was mine and mine alone to occupy. Elderhood taught me something quite different and unexpected, however. I began to feel that I no longer needed to assert my boundaries as I had in my younger years. Pretenses were of little importance to me, and I felt that I had nothing left to prove. Self-indulgent expressions of pride or bravado only served to deepen the gap that already existed between the younger generation and me.

I began to intuit that something else was coalescing within that was allowing me to release an older, more visible version of myself that had supported me while I built the earlier structures of my life. Had it not been for the children who were just not interested in the intellectual knowledge I thought I had to pass down, I might not have been so inclined to search within myself for a posture that was more fitting to their (and my) needs and pathway. It was their time. They were smart, capable, and filled with the same exuberance for life that once flowed through my veins. To give way, to witness, to honor and take pleasure in their gifts and accomplishments, and to convey confidence in their abilities to face and overcome the challenges through which I once navigated were my sacred tasks now. I was glad to just hold them with the love of my presence and quiet reassurance that the rapids of life would eventually give way to calmer waters.

It was a profound revelation to me that *all others really wanted or needed from me was my simple, loving presence.* I began to see that this was all that was ever real anyway; the rest was survival, entertainment, and grist for the mill for discerning reality from illusion. I once pondered what I wanted to leave behind in the hearts of others. I have been interested to realize that it is only, and simply, who I have become in my long journey that might be of much value to anyone. I also have been surprised to discover that the more present I am to life, and to this simple truth, the more prepared I am for wherever my journey happens to take me. I have entered a level of happiness unimaginable in my earlier years and have come to believe that *happiness is our true nature and birthright.* The wisdom we gather along the way is no more than the process of discernment that enables us to clear away the rubbish that keeps us from seeing and becoming this simple truth. If I have nothing else for others to remember me by, I hope it will be my happiness.

As I have arrived at the latter part of my life, I have found that one of the hardest parts of getting old has been my gradual loss of independence and my feeling that I might be a burden to others. The pains and emerging illnesses that naturally come with aging become so much a part of who we are that it is difficult for them not to define us over time. I have refused to align with my physical decline, however, since it does not characterize the meaning of this period of life for me. I have gradually let go of my identification with this body that has been such a friend and served me so well. I bless it as it slowly turns to dust. As my body has faded, I have felt gratified to welcome a fuller experience of my heart and my native vulnerability. Nonetheless, giving myself over to the care of others on such basic levels as I had in my infancy has been one of my remaining challenges. One of the last things to empty from my basket has been my need for respect and dignity and to be recognized as one who knows, who has lived through so much of what life has to offer up. To free myself of these last remnants of control and status and to welcome the compassion and care flowing in from others has connected me with the felt memory of my beginnings; to return full circle surprisingly has allowed me to release the remaining pain that filled my early weeks of separation that so-long colored my experience of intimacy with others.

The majority of my dear friends have now passed away, and their memories have filled my heart for many years. I will leave behind my loving wife, without whom I would have made only half of the journey, and my children and grandchildren who have filled my life with indescribable joy, heartache, and meaning. The veil that creates an illusion of separation of the here and here-after has been slowly losing its form for me. While this gives me much comfort as the time arrives for my final goodbyes, I still find that I shudder, nervously, in the presence of this experience of seeming finality. I really don't know how to say goodbye to those whose hearts will always live within mine. Maybe we do need an Angel of Death to pull us away from the grip that this life has so powerfully secured over us. Why does it require these final moments to reveal to us the enormity of the gifts that our lives have bestowed upon us?

A lifetime of re-membering, of putting together the pieces of who I am, began making possible a deepening awareness that was allowing me to release myself more fully into the vast Oneness from which I came. The dualities that are so much a part of our journey through the unfolding of consciousness were fading like the melting snow in springtime. My basket finally empty, I was feeling as if I were leaving exactly the way I came: naked, exposed, and infinitely open to the next adventure that lay ahead. In my dreaming, I could sense that the voices that lived in my heart for so long were now accompanied by hands reaching from the beyond to welcome me home after a long journey through the wonders, confusion, and pain of human life. "Thank you," I say, "Thank you!"

Winter // Author

My last weeks with Shemah transported me to a place within myself where I began to glimpse just a fragment of the reality that he was attempting to transmit. As he began to make his transition, he left me with three very important understandings that he believed were central to nurturing and sustaining our continued evolution though the seasons of living.

Shemah underscored the importance of learning to slowly and carefully unveil the light which lies at the depth of our being. There are those, like Icarus, who naively fly too quickly and closely to the sun only to find their wings singed by its overwhelming heat. There are others who strive only to peek behind the veil, satisfied with thinking of the light as that which lies unobtainably outside of their conception of self. Shemah believed that finding our way home to the ground of being was not an end-in-itself. He felt that we enter the human form for the experience and adventure, and that Self-discovery is like a slow-cooked meal or like the balanced ripening of fruit. He felt that we must learn to trust that the light of being works wisely within us to reveal itself in its own time and its own way as our lives unfold.

Shemah was also aware of just how easy it was to get caught within the rocks and eddies of our conditioning as we are carried by the currents of our life energies. He felt that, when we are navigating the great labyrinth of life, learning to discern the subtle differences between when we are caught within the rocks and when we are traveling freely along our destined path is one of our most important tasks. Powerful attachments to the security of familiar ways of thinking, feeling, and being often obscure our vision of what is constricting the free flow of our life-force. Shemah believed that until we could tell the difference between the compulsive grip of our conditioning and the organic flow of our Original Being we cannot even begin to identify the nature of the chains that bind us. *He also continued to remind me how much courage it takes to remain open to the love that is our true nature. Without this conscious, open presence, he believed, it is not possible to transcend our very formidable circumstances.*

Shemah's last gift was to help me understand that to remain attuned to the mysterious movements of life energies we must each learn to develop our deep intuitive capacities. According to him, these intuitive abilities enable us to sense their subtle movements and to "sniff out the path" ahead, as he put it. Shemah conveyed that, when we are "caught in the rocks," our life force energies slowly dwindle, creating illness and melancholy. He felt that, because of fear, loss of energy, or a need for a feeling of safety, we often hold tightly to these rocks even when a simple letting go would free and carry us to where the energies were again flowing with the waters of life. He also realized that it is very difficult for us to perceive subtleties when we make little time for spaciousness and quiet. He felt that we must slow down and quiet down for us to be able to read the "sacred text" that is always unfolding around us.

When Shemah left his body, it was clear to me that this passage was not at all an ending. Even at the moment of his death he continued the practice of "sniffing the path" ahead to where the energy was alive and moving. As he said his goodbyes, I could feel him opening intently as he anticipated his crossing from an adventure already lived to a new one awaiting his joyous eyes and loving smile.

EPILOGUE

Shemah (1927-2020)

Shemah's family arrived, having been informed of the imminence of his passing. His last days were quiet and filled with the grace of visitors who deeply loved him. His body had grown thin and frail, his face gaunt, his consciousness fading in and out as his shallow pulses warned of the final beats of a waning heart. The room was filled with flowers when I arrived, and photos of family members, particularly grandchildren, dotted every remaining corner where medical equipment and tables filled with medications did not encumber the space. Frost on the window during that cold January day shaded the view of the icicles on deciduous trees just outside. Anticipating his last moments, prayer sounded around him. Suddenly, with a gaping in-breath, he opened his eyes widely as an expression of ecstatic wonder illuminated his countenance, followed by the last out-breath that filled the room with palpable energy as his body emptied of life.

As I held his hand that day while he took his last breaths, I could see the love in his eyes as tears washed along his cheeks, knowing, somehow, that these tears reflected both grief for a well-loved life and a necessary emotional release as he began to untether from his body. His transition reminded me of the story of his father's passing and the broken hearts left behind by his early, sudden death. Shemah was not my father, and his death was not sudden, but my heart filled with grief and tore, rending wide to account for his large presence in my life and his death. I had lost an intimate, dear friend, my very own "Cornelius" who had introduced me to my Self in ways I had never before experienced.

Within days of his death, I had an early morning dream. He came to me tangibly, as real as any other time we met in this life. With warm, welcoming eyes and skin smooth and supple with renewed life, he said:

> *I'm grateful for the precious moments we spent in our frequent dialogues. I love you. Understand that what dies is never our connections to one another or our memories of shared love. What dies is our attachment to things that were never ours to possess in the first place. It is our freedom from these attachments that allows the heart to sing and the soul to open to new dimensions of joy and experience that forever expands us and brings us closer to the Source.*

After some time sitting side-by-side in tender silence, he hugged me and bid me, "Goodbye, for now," his typical loving smile letting me know that there was so much more to the story than could be revealed.

Morning arrived swiftly as I awoke in tears, viscerally knowing the truth of these words and somewhat shaken, as he had shown me what his father had revealed to him in this place in between life and death. In that moment together, I experienced how consciousness is passed from one person to another and the ethereal threads that bind us in undying lineage. I felt these threads extending from Shemah to me like pulsing arteries from the valves of the heart shunting "blood" from his circulatory system to mine. I knew then that I was next in a very long ancestry of souls poised to offer my life's energies to the following generation of "listeners" seeking, also, to remember who they are.

All Paths Lead Home

HONORARIUM
It Takes a Village

Drs Jim Neafsey, Ken Lakritz,
Huston Smith & Len Zunin
"Four Way Lunch"

Drs Frank Varela, Ken Lakritz,
Greg Matsumoto, Tom Knoblauch,
& Winston Valois
"Fellowship"

Ken & Ram Dass

Elijah Lakritz & Fr Dunstan Morrissey
"Sky Farm Hermitage"

Elijah & Ken

Robin Rosholt & Ken

Dolores Jaehrling, Jens Hansen
John Wurr and Drs Elizabeth Simpson,
Abe Levitsky, Pauline Thompson,
Tom Knoblauch, Ken Lakritz & Tim Crocker
"From *Elders on Love*"

Ken & Rajashree Maa

This book is dedicated to

The memory of
Winston Regis Valois
who taught me how to listen deeply

Lenard M. Zunin
mentor and midwife to my creative process

The memories of
My Father and My Mother
who sparked my passion about the unfolding human journey

My Wife
Robin
who shares with me the sacred alchemy of marriage

My Son
Elijah Shai Rosholt Lakritz
who continues to immerse me in the memories of childhood and beyond

A warm thank you to

Muse, Guide, Teacher
Sandra Simon
who challenged me to reach deeper to discover the full dimension of my
writing

And
Rajashree Maa (Joni Dittrich, Ph.D.)
who encouraged me to bring this work to the public

Special Thank You
to Huston Smith

Ken & Huston

Between The Words
For Huston Age 91

Layers upon layers,

Life lived in search of that which

Cannot be found…

Like concentric rings of water that ripple

Outward

Toward the fathomless

Edges of the unknowable.

It is in this place that we Meet,

Expressing that which cannot

Be spoken,

Sensing

That which cannot be touched,

Listening to that

Which cannot be heard,

Truth that can only be grasped

In ineffable, fleeting moments,

Between the words,

Between the thoughts,

Between the feelings,

In the silent, eternal present

Where God whispers

A love song

That ceaselessly pulses through the heart.

And… It is in this timeless, spaceless

Moment

That our souls meet

And our friendship becomes an

Everlasting Spark

of the Divine

Ken Lakritz

May 28, 2010

Huston Smith Archive, Syracuse University

In Memory of Dee

9-14-1928 to 8-29-2024

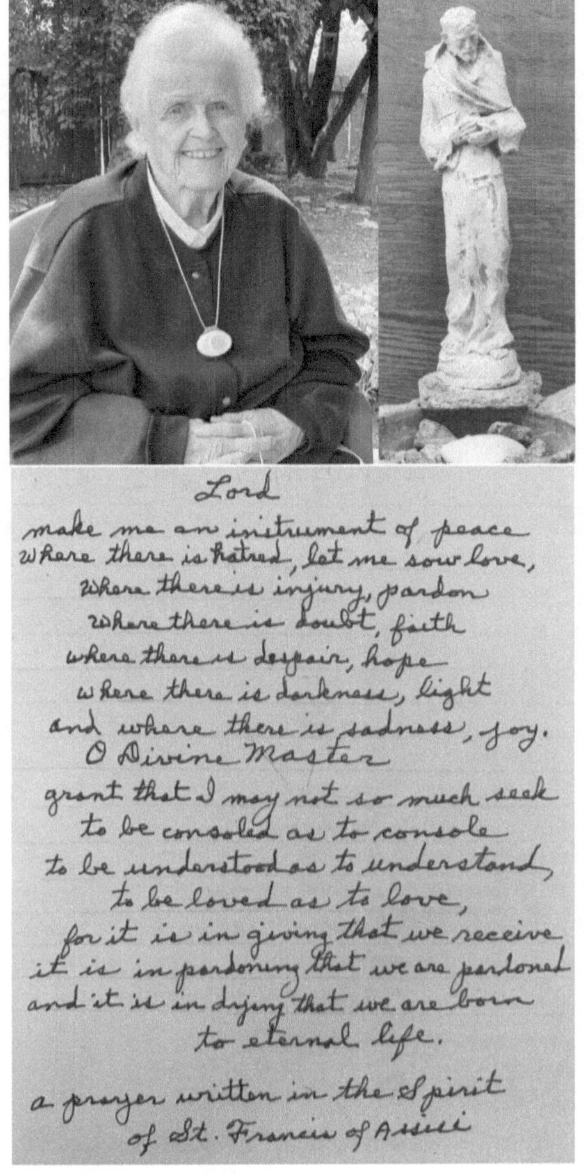

Dolores "Dee" Helen Jaehrling, former Franciscan nun

In Loving Memory
to My Father-In-Law
Robert Rosholt
2-15-1936 to 7-3-2024

"Life's a gift wrapped in strugglepaper."

FOOTNOTE BIBLIOGRAPHY

1. Shany, L., Neumann, E. (2025). *The Theory*. Chiron Publications.

2. Kabir (2004). *Kabir: Ecstatic Poems* (R. Bly, Trans.). Beacon Press.

3. Rotenberg, M. (2015). *The Psychology of TzimTzum, Self, Other, and God*. Maggid Books.

4. See #1.

5. "By ego I understand a complex of ideas which constitutes the centre of my field of consciousness and appears to possess a high degree of continuity and identity." Jung, C.G. [1921] 1971. *Psychological Types*. In *Collected Works of C.G. Jung*, vol. 6. Princeton University Press.

6. Hollis, J. (1993). *The Middle Passage: From Misery to Meaning in Midlife*. Inner City Books.

7. Jung, C.G., Adler, G., Hull, R.F.C. (1966). *Collected Works of C.G. Jung*, Volume 7: "Two Essays in Analytical Psychology". Princeton University Press.

8. Neumann, E. (1949). *The Origins and History of Consciousness*, originally published in German as *Ursprungsgeschichte des Bewusstseins* by Rascher Verlag, Zürich.

9.   See #6.

10. Mills, J. (2013). "Jung's Metaphysics". In *International Journal of Jungian Studies*, Vol. 5, No. 1: 19, 43.

11.   Huston Smith, personal communication

12. Nagarjuna (1986). *Nāgārjuna: The Philosophy of the Middle Way* (D. Kalupahana, Trans.). State University of New York Press. (Original work published ca. 150 CE)

13. Tillich, P. (1952). *The Courage to Be*. Yale University Press.

14. Mentor referred to is Fr. Dunstan Morrissey, OSB (1923-2009).

15. See #8.

16. See #1.

17. Jung, C.G. (1928). "The Relations between the Ego and the Unconscious" (R.F.C. Hull trans.). In G. Adler, M. Fordham & H. Read (Eds.), *The Collected Works of C.G. Jung*, volume 7: "Two Essays on Analytical Psychology" (p. 267). Princeton University Press.

18. Kalsched, D. (2013). *Trauma and the Soul*. Routledge.

19. See #8.

20. Jung, C.G. (1957). *The Transcendent Function* (A. R. Pope, Trans.). Zurich Students' Association, C. G. Jung Institute (pp. 23, 55).

21. Robert Bly quoting Marie-Louise Von Franz from her film *A Gathering of Men*. Moyers, B. (Producer). (1990). *A Gathering of Men* [Film]. Public Broadcasting Service.

22. Weil, S. (1952). *Gravity and Grace* (E. Crawford & M. Ruhr trans.). Routledge Classics.

23. See #8.

24. Unamuno, M. (1992). "Throw Yourself Like Seed". In R. Bly, J. Hillman & M. Meade (Eds.), *The Rag and Bone Shop of the Heart: A Poetry Anthology* (p. 234). HarperCollins Publishers.

25. Leonard M. Zunin, M.D.

26. Giovanni, N. (1975). "The Women Gather". In *The Women and the Men: Poems*. Morrow.

ABOUT THE AUTHOR

Kenneth R. Lakritz, Ph.D. is a licensed clinical psychologist with four decades of experience. Dr. Lakritz's career has taken a winding path from clinical neuropsychology through his current dedication to long-term depth psychotherapy with an alchemical, Jungian orientation. He has devoted his clinical and academic life to adult developmental challenges, both with mid- and late-life populations, and has spent many years writing on the subjects of eldering, inter-generational dialogue, and late-life development. For decades, Dr. Lakritz also has been a proponent, practitioner, and experiencer of psychedelic assisted psychotherapy, with its capacity to help us access and work with the deepest and most difficult dimensions of the psyche. He is an author of books and articles about adult development, conscious aging, and elder wisdom, including the Parabola book, *Elders on Love: Dialogues on the Consciousness, Cultivation, and Expression of Love*. Dr. Lakritz received a Doctor of Philosophy in clinical psychology from The California School of Professional Psychology, Berkeley, California, 1985.

MESSAGE FROM THE PUBLISHER

Light on Light Press produces enhanced content books spotlighting the sacred ground upon which all religious and wisdom traditions intersect; it aims to stimulate and perpetuate engaged interspiritual and perennial wisdom dialogue for the purpose of assisting the dawning of a unitive consciousness that will inspire compassionate action toward a just and peaceful world.

We are delighted to publish *Remembering Self* because it spotlights the deeper levels of the common journey connecting us all as members of the human family as we make our way through the seasons of life. This book offers valuable insights into a universal process of growth, transformation, and renewal by bringing to light many lesser-known developmental challenges at each stage of life that are meant to assist our progress in this world while preparing us for what lies beyond. The interdisciplinary and integrative approach Dr. Kenneth Lakritz applies to this exploration of the essence and meaning of life's journey offers engaging and accessible guidance to all, especially those in the helping professions.

We consider this to be a groundbreaking book in providing new depth to understanding the purpose, direction, and destination of the life course. This book is also unique in that it offers significant wisdom for navigating life's twists and turns with intentionality. It also provides many inviting, heart-opening meditations to assist and guide a developing consciousness. We welcome *Remembering Self* in taking its place among our other books that tell our timeless, universal story in which wholeness is at the very center – and periphery – of all things.

Especially in the context of Light on Light's commitment to books furthering the interspiritual paradigm – and the now famous words of Br. Wayne Teasdale (coiner of the word "Interspirituality"), "the definitive revolution is the spiritual awakening of humankind" – this volume is particularly timely, and urgent.

Managing Editors—

Kurt Johnson PhD
Robert Atkinson PhD
Chamatkara (Sandra Simon)
Nomi Naeem, MA

www.ingramcontent.com/pod-product-compliance
Lightning Source LLC
Chambersburg PA
CBHW030917060726
47591CB00005B/1574